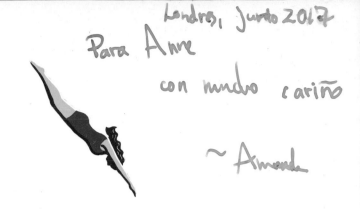

WILD swimming
Walks

28 lake, river and seaside
days out by train from London

Kenwood Ladies' Pond Association

Editor: Margaret Dickinson
Photo editor: Sarah Saunders

WILD swimming
Walks

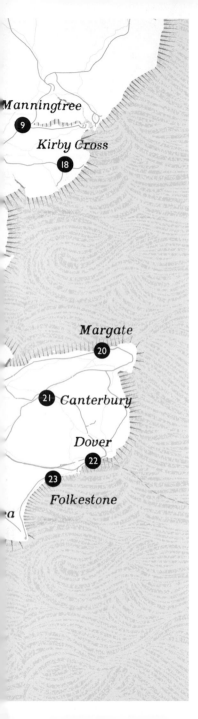

THE WALKS

No.	NAME	COUNTY	SWIMMING	TERRAIN
1	Hampstead Waters	London	Ponds and lido (£) (Lifeguarded)	Urban open space
2	Finsbury Park to Hampstead Ponds	London	Ponds (£) (Lifeguarded)	Park, urban village, urban open space
3	The Serpentine, Hyde Park	London	Lake (£) (Lifeguarded)	City streets and city park
4	Farnham to Frensham Great Pond or Bentley Station	Surrey, Hampshire	Lake and shallow river	Level and gently hilly. Woods, heathland, fields
5	Rickmansworth Circular	Hertfordshire	Lake (uncertain access) and shallow river	Level and gently hilly. Country park, fields, small woods
6	Watton-at-Stone to Hertford	Hertfordshire	River Beane. Shallow and deep places	Gently rolling. Fields, woods, urban canal towpath
7	Shepreth to Cambridge	Cambridgeshire	River Cam	Level and nearly level. Fields, riverside park, historic town streets
8	Hatfield Peverel Circular	Essex	River Chelmer	Level with some gentle hills. Fields, patches of woodland, rural towpath
9	Manningtree Circular	Essex and Suffolk	River Stour	Level and gently rolling. Fields, small woods, historic riverside
10	Hever to Leigh	Kent	River Medway	Gently rolling. Fields, woods, parkland
11	Chilworth to Guildford	Surrey	Wey Navigation	Hilly and level. Heathland, woods, fields, rural and town towpath
12	Winchfield to Hook	Hampshire	Shallow pond (uncertain access), trout stream and canal	Level and gently hilly. Fields, woods, marsh, moorland
13	Marlow Circular	Buckinghamshire	River Thames	Chalk hills and Thames Valley. Fields and woods
14	Shiplake Circular	Oxfordshire	River Thames	Chalk hills and Thames Valley. Fields and woods
15	Goring and Streatley to Cholsey	Berkshire	River Thames	Almost level. Riverside fields, patches of woodland, village roads
16	Shillingford to Didcot	Oxfordshire	River Thames	Level with a few gentle hills. Open fields and one wood
17	A Walk around Port Meadow, Oxford	Oxfordshire	River Thames	Almost level. Urban canal towpath, semi urban open spaces, fields and rural riverside
18	Kirby Cross to Walton-on-the-Naze	Essex	Sea from sandy beaches	Level with a slight hill. Open fields, resort sea front, coastal scrubland and salt marsh
19	Benfleet and Leigh-on-Sea	Essex	Estuary from sandy beach (mid to high tide)	Level with a slight hill. Fields, salt marsh and resort sea front
20	Margate to Broadstairs	Kent	Sea from sandy beaches, Sea Pool (mid to low tide)	Mainly level with slight hills. Resort sea front, semi-rural cliff
21	Canterbury to Swalecliffe	Kent	Sea from shingle beach (mid to high tide)	Part hilly, part almost level. Urban streets and paths, large woods, open fields, resort sea front
22	Dover to Deal	Kent	Sea from shingle beaches	Undulating with some steep hills. Historic city streets, resort sea front, rural chalk cliff tops
23	Folkestone to Dover	Kent	Sea from sandy and shingle beaches	Level and hilly with one very steep hill. Resort streets, seaside gardens, port sea front, wooded under cliff, open cliff tops, downland
24	Winchelsea to Rye	East Sussex	Sea from shingle beach (mid to high tide)	Hilly and level. Historic town streets, fields, patches of woodland, salt marsh, drained levels, open shore
25	Three Oaks to Hastings	East Sussex	Sea from rocky naturist beach and shingle town beach	Hilly with some steep hills and a scramble. Fields, woods, wooded under cliff, part wooded cliff tops, old town sea front
26	Berwick to Seaford	East Sussex	Sea from shingle beaches	Hilly and level with some steep hills. Fields, woods, open cliff tops, urban sea front
27	Southease to Newhaven	East Sussex	Sea from shingle beaches	Hilly and level. Open downland and open sea shore
28	Arundel to Littlehampton	West Sussex	Sea mixed shingle and sandy beach (mid to high tide only)	Mainly level. Historic streets, woods, fields, rural riverside, semi urban roads, open foreshore

TRAVEL	START POINT	END POINT	MILES	DIFFICULTY
London Transport	Hampstead Heath Overground Station	Gospel Oak Overground Station	3.5	Easy
London Transport	Finsbury Park Underground Station	Hampstead Heath Overground Station	4	Easy
London Transport	Leicester Square Underground Station	Marble Arch Underground Station	4	Easy
Train out; bus and train back or train both ways	Farnham Station	Bus stop by Frensham Pond or Bentley Station	8 or 13	Moderate/hard
London Transport or train	Rickmansworth Underground Station	Rickmansworth Underground Station	6	Easy/moderate
Train	Watton-at-Stone Station	Hertford North Station	8	Moderate
Train	Shepreth Station	Cambridge Station	9.5	Moderate
Train	Hatfield Peverel Station	Hatfield Peverel Station	8 or 11	Moderate
Train*	Manningtree Station	Manningtree Station	7.25	Moderate
Train	Hever Station	Leigh Station	7.5	Moderate
Train* out; train back	Chilworth Station	Guildford Station	8	Moderate
Train	Winchfield Station	Hook Station	11	Moderate
Train*	Marlow Station	Marlow Station	11 or 16	Moderate/hard
Train*	Shiplake Station	Shiplake Station	7	Moderate
Train	Goring and Streatley Station	Cholsey Station	4	Easy
Train and bus out; train back	Shillingford, Kingfisher Inn bus stop	Didcot Station	8.5	Moderate
Train or express bus	Oxford Station	Oxford Station	6	Easy
Train*	Kirby Cross Station	Walton-on-the-Naze Station	5 or 7.5 or 10.5	Moderate
Train	Benfleet Station	Benfleet or Leigh-on-Sea Station	4.5 or 5.5 or 8.25	Easy/moderate
Train	Margate Station	Broadstairs Station	6.5	Easy
Train out; train* back	Canterbury West Station	Chesterfield & Swalecliffe Station	8.5	Moderate
Train	Dover Priory Station	Deal Station	9.5	Moderate/hard
Train	Folkestone Central Station	Dover Priory Station	9	Moderate/hard
Train*	Winchelsea Station	Rye Station	8.5 or 10	Moderate
Train*	Three Oaks Station	Hastings Station	6.5	Moderate/hard
Train*	Berwick Station	Seaford Station	9.5	Moderate/hard
Train*	Southease Station	Newhaven Harbour Station	10	Moderate/hard
Train	Arundel Station	Littlehampton Station	10	Moderate

* journey always or sometimes requires changing trains.

INTRODUCTION

RIGHTS OF WAY AND THE RIGHT TO SWIM

*W*alking and wild swimming are among the most democratic of leisure pursuits because they are free, require no special skills or training and hardly any equipment. These advantages, however, have a flip side in that no major vested interests defend or promote them, while some are opposed to them. It is not surprising that the history of both is marked by conflict.

Today's network of walking routes is the product of a long struggle, which is not over but has been so successful that its broad aims no longer seem controversial. There was a more subversive current in the 19th and early 20th centuries, when some of the militant walkers were industrial workers and their main opponents were the owners of big rural estates. So, the Ramblers, the present-day British charity supporting walking, has its origin not only in the early walkers' clubs but also in civil disobedience, most famously the Kinder Scout Trespass of 1932 when 400 people walked up the highest peak in Derbyshire in defiance of game-keepers. Three years later, in 1935, the Ramblers' Association was formed to provide a stronger national voice for walkers, and over the years its efforts led not only to important changes in the law but to developments like the creation of national parks and long-distance walking routes.

Swimming has a less robust presence in national life, and swimming purely for pleasure in natural waters, until recently, had such a low profile it was nearly invisible. So, given that, as with walking, there are conflicts of interest, it is predictable that opportunities to swim have been shrinking. Pollution by industry, agriculture and sewage has been a major problem, although it's now reduced due to European Union environmental quality standards. Other environmental threats are not diminishing, as farmers drain ponds and various interests extract excessive quantities of water.

Some landowners don't allow swimming because they think swimmers disturb money-spinning activities like fishing or boating, and in recent years they have also been motivated by the fear that they would be liable for any injuries or deaths. Sadly, some local authorities and charitable trusts which should protect public rights of access have also cited that risk as a reason to ban swimming. Both private and public landlords justify the clampdown with misleading information about supposed hazards, the risk of drowning or catching a water-borne disease even though, for most of the dangers, the level of risk if applied to more commercial recreations would mean advising people never to ski, horse ride or play football.

Swimmers only quite recently started to assert their rights in an organised way. An important landmark was the publication in 1999 of Roger Deakin's book, *Waterlog*, an evocative account of the writer's experience of swimming his way across Britain. It reached a wide readership, drew attention to the decline in open water swimming and generated conversation, which encouraged swimmers that they were part of a potential community of interest. There followed several books of a more directly campaigning nature. The pioneer, published in 2005, was Jean Perraton's *Swimming against the Stream*. Then in 2008 two books came out which popularised the phrase 'wild swimming', Daniel Start's *Wild Swimming* and Kate Rew's *Wild Swim*. The former was the first in a series of guides to where to swim, while the latter was part guide, part autobiographical essay. Each was followed by celebrity television programmes on the BBC and ITV. Since then the subject has been taken up by other writers and broadcasters so that wild swimming, as it has since been called, now has a fairly strong presence in the media. Parallel to and linked with the media exposure, two national organisations have been campaigning: the River and Lake Swimming Association (RALSA) was formed in 2003 by two enthusiastic swimmers, Rob Fryer and Yakov Lev; and the Outdoor Swimming Society (OSS) was formed by Kate Rew in 2006. In between, an important legal victory was won in a case relating to the Mixed Pond on Hampstead Heath where swimmers wanted to swim in the winter without lifeguards. The court ruled in 2005 that the Heath management could not be prosecuted under the Health and Safety at Work Act for allowing this, a decision that suggests landlords have been worrying unnecessarily about liability.

The two wild swimming associations have similar aims but the OSS is more focused on organised swimming – fun social swims, long distance swims and races. Recently, participation in marathon swims, duathlons and triathlons has increased, probably due to the influence of the London Olympics as well as the work of the OSS. Sadly, neither the media exposure or the court case of 2005, or the resurgence of competitive outdoor swimming, has translated into significantly improved access for wild swimmers yet. As far as we know, few, if any, 'No swimming' signs have been taken down. Some lake owners who ban casual swimmers have introduced periods of organised swimming, but usually just a few hours a week and only for members of a club. This is a small advance but hardly relevant to the independent swimmer who does not ask for facilities or

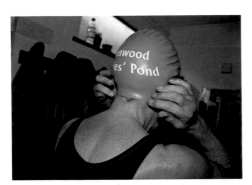

lifeguards and wants to swim spontaneously, exercising his or her discretion as to safety.

Many swimmers happily ignore 'No swimming' signs, just as walkers ignore 'No trespassers' signs on rights of way. In this book, however, we have tried to recommend only swimming places where access is not in doubt because people expecting to swim on a long walk need to be reasonably sure they can do so. Of course, a swim can never be guaranteed. The sea can be rough, a river can be in spate or depleted by drought. We can only promise that in normal conditions the swim will be more or less as described, and the walk worth doing even without the swim.

THE LONDON CONTEXT

*T*he idea for this book was seeded in conversations at Kenwood Ladies' Pond on London's Hampstead Heath, a place where we swim past banks of reeds and purple loosestrife and share the dark water with ducks, fish and the occasional heron or kingfisher. Those conversations developed into a collaborative venture supported by Kenwood Ladies' Pond Association, the organisation that represents users of the pond. The aim is partly to support the wild swimming movement, but also to share with a wider public walks with swims we have enjoyed near London – walks that we hope will tempt those unsure about cold water as well as the dedicated wild swimmer.

London is a city famed for its green spaces but not generally thought of as a centre for country walking, still less swimming. Yet one of the capital's delights is, paradoxically, getting out of it, and the day trip – the dash beyond the smoke – has long been a part of London life, reflected in the growth of nearby resorts. After clean air, water was a big attraction, evident in the siting of resorts by mineral springs or the sea and in relics of resort architecture such as regency bathhouses or modernist lidos. The quick dip on a country walk

leaves no such physical record, but a smattering of literary references connect walking and a love of nature with swimming. Byron, Wordsworth, Robert Bridges, Virginia Woolf and Iris Murdoch are a few of the most famous writers who were drawn to the countryside and to swimming.

A swim is cooling and cleansing but has a sensuous appeal beyond the merely practical: the silky touch of water, the strange sensation of floating, the cold shock and warm afterglow. Besides such animal pleasures there are aesthetic ones to do with being literally immersed in the landscape. I would hesitate to suggest, as some swimmers do, that cold water has mystical benefits but I am sure it has psychological ones. Many of us who swim regularly outdoors think it helps us through difficult times.

Hampstead Heath and the ponds are especially valued because London is so vast that anywhere comparable is hard to reach. We know getting out of London to walk or swim can seem daunting despite the plethora of information available. I felt trapped when I first moved to the capital even though I was a practised reader of maps and timetables. Growing up in Bristol I used to go for a walk or bike ride most weekends and would swim in any bit of water on the way that looked adequately clean. But Bristol, before the motorways enclosed it, was a city you could easily walk out of, and if you wanted to go further afield you knew the country buses went from one central bus station. London, 16 times bigger, was far more complex and I felt oppressed by the miles of bricks and tarmac, which stood between the open fields and me. Then a friend

started to arrange walks. Every so often he would tell us where to meet and we'd take a train, get off at some little station, walk miles to another little station and, preferably, pause at a pub in between. Suddenly London seemed less claustrophobic.

Those long-ago walks helped me to appreciate that a dense transport network compensates for the great size of London's built-up area, a network that radiates outwards and puts within relatively easy reach 10 counties and a remarkable range of landscapes containing many rivers and long stretches of coast.

The South East lacks any very rugged or remote areas, although 200 years ago parts of the Weald, the heaths along the Greensand Way and some stretches of coast were considered wild and dangerous. Even now, in the gathering dusk or during a bad storm, they can still feel inhospitable, but in normal conditions there are too many roads, pockets of suburbia and tourist attractions to imagine getting seriously lost, dying of exposure or meeting a witch. A shortage of wilderness, however, is offset by a richness of culture. Being near the capital and Canterbury, the centre of ecclesiastical power, having numerous ports and being crossed by navigable rivers, the region is marked by centuries of intense commercial, political and religious life, which has left a particularly dense collection of relics. Artists and writers have been prominent among the Londoners who acquired houses in the nearby countryside, with the result that nowhere, except perhaps the Lake District, has been so intensely celebrated in literature and art. Among the many delights of these walks is entering the space of familiar artworks, strolling through a Constable painting by the Stour or climbing the Downs into a Paul Nash landscape, for instance.

We offer this book as a small contribution to support all those working to ensure that future generations can enjoy these pleasures.

Margaret Dickinson

WATER SAFETY

*S*wimming in open water is not dangerous as long as you follow reasonable precautions, are aware of possible risks and know your own limits. Remember that most of the swims on these walks are in the countryside where there are no lifeguards, no facilities and no one but you to decide whether the conditions are safe.

- Avoid getting too cold. Be cautious about length of time in the water, especially if you are not acclimatised. If in doubt get out. If you feel cold after swimming dress quickly, put on an extra layer, start walking again and, if your fingers are numb, exercise them.

- Early signs of hypothermia include extreme shivering and numb fingers or toes; more serious ones include feeling sleepy and dizzy. If you have symptoms leave the water, put on layers of warm, dry clothing and sip a warm drink. For mild symptoms keep active, but for more serious ones avoid activity, stay quiet but awake, and in the unlikely event of a hot shower being available, avoid it.

- Never jump or dive unless you have checked that the water is deep enough, there are no underwater obstructions, and that you will be able to get out of the water.

- Try to avoid swimming alone in deep water.

- Try to avoid weeds, but if you swim into them, swim through them using your arms or turn around slowly.

- Look out for blue-green algae, which can occur in lowland lakes or ponds, usually in summer. It may appear as a turquoise or greenish scum and some kinds are toxic, can be an irritant, or make you sick if you swallow it. Try to avoid it by swimming in a part of the lake without it or swimming away from it.

- Avoid swimming with an open wound or cut.

- Weil's disease can be caught in urban waters from rats' urine but is very uncommon. Avoid standing around in mud. Avoid entering water where livestock trample the bank.

- In rivers always check which way the water is running (it can be deceptive if a wind is blowing). Swim upstream as it will be easy to return. In powerful rivers, make sure there is somewhere to get out in case you are carried downstream.

- When sea swimming always check tide times and conditions – if in doubt seek local advice.

- Make sure you can swim in both directions parallel to the shore (in case there is a current) and don't swim too far out.

- If caught in a rip current that takes you out to sea, don't panic. Swim out of it parallel to the beach, then aim for the shore or use the waves to help you bodysurf back.

- Generally, the fastest tidal flows are in the middle hours of the tide so if in doubt swim at high or low tides. Tide cycles repeat every 13 or so hours, so the tide is usually approximately an hour later each day.

- It can be difficult to get out of the sea on a shelving beach where the surf breaks quickly and heavily onto shingle with a powerful undertow. Aim to land behind the breaking wave, or find a more gently sloping part of the beach.

- If you wear a swimming hat choose a brightly coloured one that will make you easy to spot in the water.

- Look out for boats and surfers.

Acknowledgments: Daniel Start (Wild Swimming, Wild Swimming Hidden Beaches), Kate Rew (Wild Swim)

EQUIPMENT

*E*ssential kit includes towel and swim gear unless the swim spot is secluded. Some swimmers take a sports towel or a fine cotton sari, which is light, provides changing cover and dries quickly. For shingle beaches light rubber shoes or sandals can be useful. Carry an extra layer or two of clothing for after the swim.

Good boots will support your feet and keep them dry. Leg coverings can protect you from stings and bites; loose trousers that dry quickly are practical, along with a sun hat for summer days, a fleece for cold days and always a waterproof. Aside from that, choose your clothing to fit the weather and the season, remembering that people have walked long distances for millennia in their ordinary clothes. Hiking sticks can be helpful on rough terrain or steep descents, as in the Downs and Weald walks, but you can often improvise from cuttings lying about in woods or hedgerows.

The directions and route maps should enable you to find your way without an additional map or GPS, but we strongly advise you to carry the relevant Ordnance Survey (OS) map as it can help you find your way back onto the route if you make a mistake, it places the walk in the landscape and gives you the flexibility to vary the route. A compass is not generally needed but most smartphones have one that you can use in conjunction with a map.

GETTING THERE

*W*e have included only walks accessible by public transport because we want them to be available to everyone, it is better for the environment, plus it offers a chance to see the countryside and many small stations en route, rather than sit in traffic. If you prefer to drive most of the walks can be accessed by car, with the circular ones or those starting and finishing on the same railway line the best options.

Always check National Rail Enquiries for train times and details of line closures that often take place at the weekend. Transport for London has information for travel within London. For the few walks that use a country bus or where a bus can shorten the walk, check the bus company's website or ring them for details.

The main ways to get cheap train tickets are:

OFF-PEAK DAY RETURNS: At weekends and between certain hours on weekdays you can buy day returns costing the same or little more than a single. Do check that the ticket covers both outward and return routes as some are restricted to particular companies.

BOOK IN ADVANCE: This can bring big savings but locks you into a date at least three weeks in advance, and most of the really cheap tickets are on trains in the middle of the day.

USE A RAILCARD: Most useful are the Network Railcard for the South East, the Family Railcard and the Senior Railcard. If you have a Freedom Pass or an Oyster Card with free weekend travel, you save money by booking from the boundary zone instead of the terminus.

GROUP TICKETS: Most rail companies offer discounts for group travel. For large groups of 10 or more it is advisable to make inquiries in advance from the relevant rail company. For small groups from three to nine tickets can be bought on the day and it is best to ask at the ticket office for the best tickets for the number of people travelling, mentioning whether any of them hold railcards.

WEATHER AND SEASONS

There is no need to wait for a hot, sunny day to try out one of these walks and swims. Water temperature depends more on the weather during the preceding days than on the day itself, and water can actually feel colder on a hot day because of the contrast. Cool days are better for walking, and swimming on a walk is quite different from swimming after sitting still because the walking warms you up both before and afterwards.

For similar reasons the walks can be done over a fairly long season. Even people who regard the swimming season as July and August can enjoy a quick dip on a walk during any reasonably good weather from May to early October. And it is

possible to enjoy swimming for a much longer season; most of the contributors to this book swim outdoors all year and the swims in it were done between March and November. The reason none were done further into winter is partly because swimming in the cold in an unknown place far from shelter is not the same as swimming in a familiar place near to coffee, toast and central heating, but also because the short days make the longer and more distant walks less attractive. The sea, which takes a long time to cool down, can be pleasant even into December.

A good rule of thumb is go in if the water appeals, whatever the weather or season. Always take a costume and towel just in case.

HOW TO USE THE BOOK

*T*here are three parts to each walk: key information including distance, how to get there, where to eat and places of interest; a general description of the walk and swim; and detailed directions of the route. The numbers in the description refer to the numbers on the accompanying route map.

Distances are in miles and usually given to 0.5 of a mile, occasionally to 0.25. They are roughly measured, not adjusted for relief and do not take account of every wriggle of a footpath.

Times always refer to walking time and are, of course, approximate. Two abbreviations are used throughout, OS for Ordnance Survey and FP for footpath.

Most of the routes were walked specifically for the book at least twice by different people. The few walked only once are comparatively straightforward and had been walked previously some time in the past by at least one of us.

Despite the checks, there is no guarantee that all route details will prove accurate because some will almost certainly change with time: a stile replaced with a gate, a signpost blown down, a house renamed. In some cases

we found such changes even in a few months between first walking and then testing a route. Be aware that anything that looks very new may not have been there when the walk was written up.

Unless stated, the contributors tried out the swims mentioned, but swims are prone to change with seasons and weather. Do not assume that conditions will be exactly as described.

The descriptions reflect the particular experiences of the contributors. Most were written mainly by the first walker, with amendments from subsequent walkers. The names of the contributors are at the end of each walk in the order in which they did the walk. More than two names does not mean the walk is complicated, but more probably that the first or second walker suggested changing the route which then had to be tried out and tested.

DOWNLOADABLE route information, to print out or to transfer to your smart phone, can be found at wildthingspublishing.com/kenwood. Insert the last two words of each chapter introduction, with no spaces or capitals. E.g. for Walk 1 go to wildthingspublishing.com/kenwood/trainthere

KLPA AND THE HAMPSTEAD HEATH SWIMMING PONDS

*K*enwood Ladies' Pond Association (KLPA) takes its name from the pond. In practice, most members talk of the 'women's pond' but when the Association's name was discussed in 2012 a majority wanted to keep the familiar name and acronym with their historical resonances.

The KLPA represents users of the Ladies' Pond and was created in 1985 when swimmers thought the future of swimming on the Heath was under threat. The key purpose of the KLPA is to negotiate and, if necessary, fight to protect all that we love about the pond. Aside from this, it is a social organisation and provides a framework for swimmers to meet and share activities such as informal excursions. There have been walks, bike rides and train or bus trips to swim around the country, including a delightful swim in much-missed author Roger Deakin's moat, a swim with Rob Fryer at Farleigh and many more, with particular affection for the Margate sea pool.

The KLPA organises events such as the New Year's Day swim at the pond, and in the early autumn a breakfast get-together to encourage swimmers to swim on into the winter. Before the present book project, KLPA itself published two books: *Early History of the Kenwood Ladies' Pond* and *The Hungry Winter Swimmer*, a cookbook with recipes interspersed with advice, poems and essays produced to encourage winter swimming. The KLPA was deeply involved in the making of the film *City Swimmers* during the 2004/5 campaigns to keep the swimming ponds open.

The immediate context for the formation of the KLPA was a time of political change when the Prime Minister, Margaret Thatcher, was intent on abolishing the Greater London Council (GLC), which managed Hampstead Heath, but the fears

of the time were also fuelled by history and folk memory. The Heath and its ponds has long been a focus of conflict between the people who use them on the one hand, and landowners, developers and managers on the other.

In the 19th century there was a real danger that the land now preserved as open space would be built over. A turning point occurred in 1871 when, after years of campaigning, the Hampstead Heath Act was passed. This allowed a public body, then the Metropolitan Board of Works, to purchase part of the present Hampstead Heath and required it not only to keep the land unenclosed, but to preserve the landscape 'in its natural aspect and state'. This Act still provides the basis for the legal status of the Heath and has often been cited during subsequent campaigns to preserve the Heath, enlarge it and protect public rights of access. A leading role in such campaigns has been played by the Heath and Hampstead Society, founded in 1897 and still active.

The ponds were then, as they are now, greatly valued both for their beauty and for opportunities to swim, paddle and fish. The history of swimming in them is somewhat sketchy, but most accounts agree that the first official swimming place was the Mixed Pond, and that by 1870 a man with a boat was employed to try to prevent drowning accidents. Thereafter, records become more numerous and tell us that Highgate Men's Pond opened in 1893 and Kenwood Ladies' in 1926, while before 1926 certain times were reserved for women at the Mixed Pond and later on at both the Mixed and the Men's.

This is the documented story, but how far people kept to the specified places and times is hard to tell. Indeed, one of the author's aunts used to reminisce that as a girl she would walk from her home in Highbury to swim in the ponds, a story that refers to a time long before 1926 and probably before 1905, but includes no mention of women's days, suggesting instead casual, unsupervised swimming from the banks.

Long after mixed bathing became the norm elsewhere, segregated swimming continued on the Heath, at first perhaps because of inertia, but by the 1970s because it was popular. Women loved Kenwood Ladies' Pond and their wish to keep it as women's space aroused little opposition because there was a pond for men, one for mixed swimming and also a lido, opened in 1938 during the great age of lido building.

Apart from the gender segregation, a long-standing feature of swimming culture on the Heath is winter swimming. People swim all year in the ponds and lido, and the four swimming places between them serve several hundred regular winter swimmers, not counting those who plunge in only for special events like the Christmas races at the Men's Pond.

The anxieties of the mid 1980s were not specially related to swimming, but were about the Heath as a whole, which since 1889 had been managed by the London County Council and its successor, the Greater London Council. There had been at least one significant conflict over management plans, but the fact that these public bodies were democratically elected was thought to provide some accountability, which was lost after the abolition of the GLC. Then the open spaces previously managed by the GLC in Hampstead were divided: Kenwood House and grounds was taken over by English Heritage, an executive non-departmental public body of the British Government, while the rest of the Heath became the responsibility of the City of London Corporation, an ancient body elected not by the people of London, but by an electorate dominated by representatives of City businesses.

The City very soon introduced significant changes in management practices, but at first none that impacted specifically on swimmers. Then in 2003 there began a period of friction over opening hours and restrictions on winter swimming. These led to the dispute, mentioned in the introduction, when swimmers proposed a winter swimming club, the City of London refused citing health and safety legislation, the swimmers challenged the decision in court, and won.

While this dispute was simmering, in the autumn of 2004 swimmers were presented with a more serious challenge when the City suddenly threatened to close the Mixed Pond permanently. These events proved the wisdom of forming the KLPA. The Mixed Pond then had no association of users and at the time of the announcement was closed for the winter. So, KLPA was in the best position to respond and the members did so vigorously. They were angry on behalf of Mixed Pond swimmers, but also angry because it was seen as a first step

in attacking the tradition of a women's space. The closure of the Mixed Pond would clearly weaken the case for segregation in the remaining ponds.

Soon swimmers from the Men's Pond, the Mixed and even the lido also began to mobilise and an umbrella group, The United Swimmers' Association of Hampstead Heath, helped coordinate a campaign strongly supported by other Heath users and sympathisers. The City eventually backed down after suffering a storm of bad publicity.

Once the threat of closure was withdrawn good relations were restored between the City and swimmers, but memories of the conflict were rekindled in 2011 when the City announced a proposal to commission major engineering work to strengthen the dams in both chains of ponds in order to comply with the Reservoirs Acts of 1975 and 2010. There followed a long period during which plans were developed in consultation with interested organisations deemed to be stakeholders. Eventually the Heath and Hampstead Society decided to oppose the plan, a decision supported by other local associations including the KLPA and the associations that by then had been formed for the Men's Pond and Mixed Pond.

Key reasons for opposition are that the works planned will detract permanently from the natural aspect of the landscape, and that they are thought to be on a scale that is not justified by the interests of safety, nor necessary to comply with the

the Acts. A factor in the dispute is that the 2010 Act requires that dams be 'safe' but leaves an engineer to define the standard of safety. The City's engineer set a standard based on the concept of a probable maximum flood, calculated in such a way that the likelihood of it occurring is 400,000:1.

Objectors have pointed out that, apart from the extreme odds against such an event, if it were to occur much of London would be under water long before the dams would be at risk. The Heath and Hampstead Society eventually challenged the City by taking the case to judicial review, but just as this book went to press the judge decided in favour of the City. It therefore seems likely that the works will go ahead despite opposition, and in that case readers should be warned that considerable parts of Walk 1 and small sections at the end of Walk 2 might be inaccessible for periods during 2015 and 2016. When the work is finished the route of Walk 1 should be roughly as described, although the landscape will have changed so much that some sections may not quite match the directions. The end of Walk 2 will also be through a changed landscape, but the route should be little affected and so remain easy to follow.

Lakes & Ponds

A quality shared by the many varied stretches of fresh water called lakes or ponds is their stillness, a calm untroubled by waves or currents. This makes them the most predictable kind of open water to swim in, and often, after some summer sunshine, the warmest.

These are good reasons to begin the book with them and another, because our focus is the South East, is that for most people in the region the closest places to wild swim are ponds. All but one of the swims in this section can be reached by the London tube network, while the Serpentine is so central that it is just a short stroll from Oxford Street. Most of these walks are therefore town walks, easy to do and full of interest. The walk from Farnham is, however, a particularly good and varied country walk with a river as well as a pond along the way.

This section is much shorter than the others, not because the countryside around London lacks ponds – maps abound with promising blue patches – but because, on investigation, rather few offer reliable, trouble-free swimming. Almost all are manmade, usually built as reservoirs or the result of mineral extraction, and can be inclined to silt up and become choked with weeds, or suffer from blue-green summer algae if left unmanaged. More significantly, their owners tend to be extra proprietorial, keen to reserve the waters for fishing or other water sports, and fence off their water or line it with aggressive 'No swimming' signs.

The ponds we include are selected from many more where in fact people do swim but defy the 'No swimming' signs and take their chances. With the exception of Bury Lake, our ponds are all ones where swimming is permitted and serious problems with water quality are rare.

HAMPSTEAD WATERS, HAMPSTEAD HEATH

A short walk on Hampstead Heath taking in some of its wildest, wooded areas, exploring all its bathing places and offering three swims.

*T*he bathing ponds on Hampstead Heath belong to two chains of ponds fed from different streams. This walk follows the Hampstead chain upstream then crosses the watershed to follow the Highgate chain downstream. Unfortunately, major engineering works are planned along the route so during parts of 2015 and 2016 walkers may have to weave their way around building sites. Details about the plans and opposition to them can be found in the introduction to this book, page 22-23.

Despite their natural appearance, the ponds are artificial, created as reservoirs between the end of the 17th century and the beginning of the 19th century. They have all evolved since then and each has its own individual character and particular permitted uses. Some are known by names and others by numbers. The Hampstead chain starts from the bottom with three ponds separated from each other only by causeways ❶: Hampstead Number 1 Pond, especially popular for watching waterfowl; Hampstead Number 2 Pond, where fishing is allowed; and then the Mixed Bathing Pond, a triangle of water edged by trees on the upper two sides. Above the Mixed Pond is a secluded, wooded valley where two streams meet, one flowing from Viaduct Pond and the other from the Vale of Health Pond. The viaduct after which the former is called looks like a decorative folly but was built in 1844 in anticipation of a housing project by Thomas Maryon Wilson, Lord of the Manor of Hampstead and one of the most determined developers against whom preservationists campaigned.

From the Vale of Health ❹ the walk crosses a wooded ridge and enters the landscaped grounds of Kenwood House ❺, which is free to visit and full of great paintings including a Rembrandt,

INFORMATION

DISTANCE: 3.5 miles.
TIME: 2 hours.
MAP: OS Landranger 176 (West London); OS Explorer 173 (London North); London A to Z.
START POINT: Hampstead Heath Overground Station, South End Green.
END POINT: Gospel Oak Overground Station or Highgate Road bus stop.
PUBLIC TRANSPORT: To South End Green take the London Overground, buses 24, 46, 168 and C11, or Northern line to Belsize Park and walk about 15 minutes. From Gospel Oak take London Overground; from Highgate Road buses C11, C2 and 214.
SWIMMING: In Hampstead Mixed Pond, Kenwood Ladies' Pond or Highgate Men's Pond; Parliament Hill Lido. Charges (2014): £2 (£1 concession) for ponds; £5.50 (£3.50 concession) for the Lido.
PLACES OF INTEREST: Kenwood House and grounds; The Vale of Health.
REFRESHMENTS: Pubs and cafés in South End Green; Kenwood Brew House (NW3 7JR, tel 020 8348 1286), Kenwood House; Parliament Hill Café (NW5 1QR, tel 020 7485 6606) near the Lido; cafés, restaurants and pubs in Swain's Lane and Highgate Hill.

a Vermeer and some of Angelica Kauffman's grand classical scenes (a genre of painting considered at the time unsuitable for women artists).

At the top of the Highgate chain are two ornamental lakes overlooked by Kenwood House, Wood Pond and Thousand Pound Pond. A stream runs from them back into Hampstead Heath and down to the Stock Pond, which is particularly lovely on a dull day in late summer or autumn when the trees are in leaf but the light is soft. Separated by a stretch of woodland is the most important pond for us, Kenwood Ladies' Pond ❼. The view from it looking downstream is of the Bird Sanctuary Pond, important for the boggy habitat round its edges and the many birds that nest there, including kingfishers and a pair of swans.

Below it is the Model Boating Pond, used now more for fishing than sailing model boats. This pond will be the one most altered if the proposed engineering works go ahead, because the dam will be extended substantially and the pond enlarged and reshaped. Below the Boating Pond lies the Men's Pond ❽, the largest of all the swimming places, then Highgate Number 1 Pond, the preferred place for dogs to swim.

Parliament Hill Lido ❾, at the end of our walk, is a large rectangle of bright turquoise water surrounded by a classic 1930s style structure of red brick, concrete and glass, looking as defiantly artificial as the ponds look natural. In 2005 it was refurbished, made shallower and relined in steel. Some people regret the loss of the old diving boards while others wish modernisation had advanced further to include a heating system. In recent years it has become increasingly popular, especially with families and long-distance swimmers who train there.

DIRECTIONS

❶ HAMPSTEAD NO 1 AND NO 2 PONDS

On leaving Hampstead Heath Overground Station, cross South Hill Park to take the path ahead uphill under trees to the Heath and past a large pond on the right, Hampstead Number 1 Pond. Continue past a narrow, tree-lined causeway and Hampstead Number 2 Pond on your right. Turn right to cross the causeway between Number 2 Pond on the right and the Mixed Pond on the left. At the end of the causeway turn left on a path with the fence

of the Mixed Pond on the left. This leads to the pond entrance and the first swim.
0.5 miles

❷ FROM THE MIXED POND

After swimming, leave the pond and turn sharp left onto an earth path with the pond enclosure on the left. At the end of the enclosure the path divides. Avoid a narrow branch straight on and take the better marked one veering slightly right uphill. On reaching a surfaced path turn left to walk above the stream valley,

with a grassy space, the football pitch, on your right. An avenue crosses the path; turn left down it. At the bottom of the hill turn off right on an earth path which rises slightly, leaving a small stream on your left, to reach Viaduct Pond.
0.75 miles

❸ VIADUCT POND TO THE VALE OF HEALTH

Turn left along the bank with the pond on the right and take a barely visible path along the lower edge of a sloping meadow with brambles to the left. At the corner of the meadow the path appears to end, but in fact drops steeply downwards through bushes and crosses a little stream by a low wooden bridge. It then winds up through woods to reach a partially surfaced level track. Turn right to find the Vale of Health Pond on your left, the highest pond of the chain.

1 mile

4 THE WATERSHED

Where the pond ends continue past some of the houses of the Vale of Health settlement and some caravans. The track then leads quite steeply uphill to a grassy, open area. At a path junction, follow the path with woods on the left and the grassy space on your right. At the end of the open space the path plunges into woods and wanders along slightly up and down until you come to a place where there are paths in all directions. Veer left and you should shortly see some railings, which mark the boundary between Hampstead Heath and the grounds of Kenwood House. When you reach a gap in the railings go through it.

1.5 miles

5 KENWOOD

Follow the gravel path to the left to reach another grassy area with patches of trees on the right. The little white house ahead and slightly to the left is the Old Dairy of Kenwood House. Shortly before the Dairy the path forks; take the right fork to a gate where you enter the grounds of Kenwood House (the large white building ahead). Here you have a choice. (a) Turn right and walk down to the first ponds of the Highgate chain, then turn left to walk beside the ponds, the second of which appears to be crossed by a white bridge. At a surfaced path, turn right as if to cross the bridge, which will be revealed as a fake, built for effect on the pond bank. (b) Walk on towards Kenwood House and along the terrace from where you see the ponds below across a sloping meadow. Follow the path round to the right and down to rejoin the pond-side route.

2 miles

CORPORATION OF LONDON

WOMEN ONLY

MEN NOT ALLOWED BEYOND THIS POINT

PUBLIC TOILETS 200M

➏ TO THE LADIES' POND

The path goes through a wood with a fence on your right, past a great tree and then slightly uphill. Ignore various turnings and continue more or less straight ahead to a gate out of the wood and back into Hampstead Heath. Turn left downhill on a surfaced path towards trees surrounding a small pond known as the Stock Pond. Pass the pond on your left then turn right at a T-junction along a rough road overhung with trees and edged on the right by railings and on the left by a fence concealing large houses. This is Millfield Lane. Shortly on the right is the entrance to Kenwood Ladies' Pond where women can have a second swim.

2.25 miles

➐ TO THE MEN'S POND

On leaving the Ladies' Pond turn right and walk on along Millfield Lane from where you may glimpse the Bird Sanctuary Pond on your right through trees. Just before reaching a road take a path branching off right downhill to a causeway between the Bird Sanctuary Pond on the right and the Model Boating Pond on the left. Before the causeway turn left along the edge of the Model Boating Pond with the water on the right. At the end of the pond cross a path which, to the right, leads over the causeway between the Model Boating Pond and the Men's Pond. Go on to the entrance of the Men's Pond, where men can have their second swim.

2.5 miles

➑ HIGHGATE NUMBER 1 POND

Continue with the Men's Pond on your right and turn right below the dam then left on a surfaced path to pass Highgate Number 1 Pond, on the left. You can finish the walk here by turning left to Highgate Road.

3 miles

➒ THE LIDO TO GOSPEL OAK STATION

To visit Parliament Hill Lido, carry straight on instead of turning left. Turn right at a T-junction by a children's area on the left, a café on the right and lavatories ahead. Shortly after the café turn left towards the brick walls of the Lido where you can have another swim if it is before 6.30pm. Leave the Heath by the entrance just past the Lido and turn right under the railway bridge to reach Gospel Oak station.

3.5 miles

Margaret Dickinson and Emma Beatrice Clark.

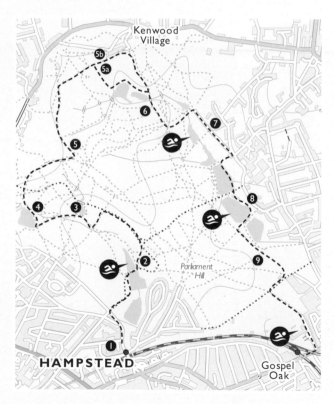

33

Walk 2

FINSBURY PARK TO HAMPSTEAD PONDS

This is an easy and surprisingly peaceful walk, incorporating a wood, historic Highgate and the most magical outdoor swimming spaces in the city.

*A*fter starting in busy, dirty, siren-shrieking Finsbury Park you quickly join a tranquil but well used path, Parkland Walk ❶. This linear green way follows a disused railway line, which once linked Finsbury Park to Alexandra Palace and was finally closed in 1970. Walking along here in the spring the sides of the path were alive with luscious green grasses, elderflowers and cow parsley. In autumn there are good blackberries to harvest. Remnants of the railway scatter the path, some overgrown, others vibrant with graffiti.

The route leaves Parkland Walk near Jacksons Lane arts venue ❷, housed in a converted church and known for innovative work in theatre, dance and contemporary circus.

On the way to Highgate, pause at Kingsley Place ❷ to enjoy the fabulous view south over London and note the house with the blue plaque commemorating Mary Kingsley, traveller and ethnologist. Soon afterwards you reach the delights of Highgate Village ❸ with its much-loved charity shops, attractive Georgian buildings and tempting pubs and eateries.

Highgate's Pond Square ❸ is a remnant of Highgate Green where there were once two ponds, made into one and then filled in and paved over in the mid 19th century. The main green area in Highgate now is that facing the elegant houses of The Grove, where Samuel Taylor Coleridge spent the last 15 years of his life at number 3 and Yehudi Menuhin once lived at number 2. No 3 was also the home of the writer JB Priestley in the 1930s and was recently bought by Kate Moss.

After dropping down from Highgate the route approaches the ponds along Millfield Lane, earlier famous as Nightingale

INFORMATION

DISTANCE: 4 miles.
TIME: 2 hours.
MAP: OS Landranger 176 (West London); OS Explorer 173 (London North); London A–Z.
START POINT: Finsbury Park Underground Station.
END POINT: Hampstead Heath Overground Station.
PUBLIC TRANSPORT: Victoria and Piccadilly lines to Finsbury Park Station; numerous buses. From Hampstead South End Green: London Overground; buses 24, 46, 168 and C11; walk to Belsize Park tube for the Northern line.
SWIMMING: Kenwood Ladies' Pond or Highgate Men's Pond, both open all year. Mixed Pond, open May to September. All have lifeguards and charge £2 (£1 concession) day entry fee. Check www.cityoflondon.gov.uk or phone 020 7485 3873 for opening times and season ticket details.
PLACES OF INTEREST: Finsbury Park; Parkland Walk; Jacksons Lane arts venue (269A Archway Road, N6 5AA, tel 020 8340 5226); Highgate Village.
REFRESHMENTS: Shops and cafés near Finsbury Park station; Finsbury Park café at the north end of the park off Endymion Road (N4 4LX, tel 020 8880 2681); pubs, cafés and restaurants in Highgate Village and South End Green.

Lane ❹ along which Coleridge and Keats, among many others, have walked. The lane may be the last in London from which you can see the stars at night, because it is unlit. Long may it remain free from light pollution.

This walk eventually leads to the ponds described in Walk 1 and so breaks the rule followed elsewhere that each walk offers different swims. We make this a special case because the swimming is exceptional and extremely accessible. The routes over the Heath are different but there is no need to repeat the information about the Heath given in Walk 1, so the description here ends with arrival at Hampstead Heath.

DIRECTIONS

❶ PARKLAND WALK
Leave Finsbury Park Station from the Station Place exit, cross Stroud Green Road and turn left, then right to take the path into Finsbury Park between the bridge and Rowan's Bowling Alley. Follow the path along the western edge of Finsbury Park until you see the sign to Highgate to the right of the narrow metal-sided footbridge over the railway. Cross the bridge and take the path off it to the right. You are now in Parkland Walk, which in a mile-and-a-half will bring you out just below Highgate Underground Station.
2 miles

❷ TO HIGHGATE
As you emerge from the path onto Holmesdale Road turn right to reach Archway Road, then right again, and walk up the hill, crossing the Archway Road at the traffic lights. Here you will see the famous Jacksons Lane arts venue. Walk up

Jacksons Lane, and at the T-junction turn left into Southwood Lane. Pause at Kingsley Place for the view.
2.5 miles

❸ HIGHGATE VILLAGE AND THE GROVE
There is a mini-roundabout ahead. Cross straight over and turn left along Highgate High Street to enjoy Highgate Village. Turn first right along South Grove and into Pond Square, passing on the left the Highgate Literary and Scientific Institute. Turn right when you reach The Old Hall in front of The Flask pub and cross over the road ahead. Walk down past a 'No Entry' sign and between two iron railing-fenced grassy areas and turn right into The Grove. Just beyond a rather curious single storey structure at 9D The Grove, turn left into Fitzroy Park. It is marked 'Private' and has an automatic barrier but pedestrians can enjoy a further traffic-free (more or less)

route towards the Ladies' and Men's Ponds.

❹ THE LADIES' POND
Follow Fitzroy Park to the T-junction with Merton Lane and turn sharp right into Millfield (or Nightingale) Lane, semi-surfaced and often muddy. Soon on the left you will see the gate to the Ladies' Pond.

❺ THE MEN'S POND
For the Men's Pond go back to the junction with Fitzroy Park and Merton Lane. When a path branches off to the right onto the Heath, follow it downhill to a little causeway with the Bird Sanctuary Pond on the right and the Model Boating Pond on the left. Turn left before the Boating Pond and walk along the edge with the water on the right. The Men's Pond is the large one below the Boating Pond and the gate is on the right-hand side.
3 miles

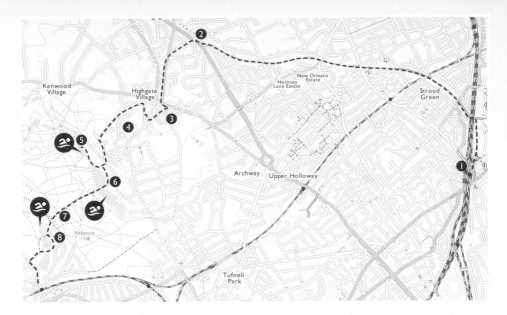

⑥ ACROSS THE CAUSEWAY AND UP THE HILL

To reach the Mixed Pond cross the causeway between the Model Boating Pond and the Men's Pond and follow the path straight up the hill with an ancient hedgerow and stream on your left. Before you reach the top turn around and look back towards the spire of Highgate Church and the ponds below. (Sometimes in the early morning you can look at this view and neither see another human being nor smell car exhaust fumes.)

⑦ THE MIXED POND

At the hill brow carry straight on over, ignoring a tarmac path to the left. When you hit a T-junction of paths turn left, then immediately right down a path with shallow steps. Below to your right is the entrance to the Mixed Pond.

3.5 miles

⑧ TO SOUTH END GREEN

On leaving the Mixed Pond, follow the path beside the Pond to the causeway. Turn right to cross and then left to descend past the lower ponds of the Hampstead chain on a path that ends at South End Green. On your left is Hampstead Heath Overground Station and, beyond, a choice of bus routes.

4 miles

Mary Cane, Shula Hawes, Jo Goldsworthy.

Walk 3

THE SERPENTINE, HYDE PARK

A swim in London's central park, passing the palaces of power and some key sites of popular protest.

*T*he Serpentine is home to the oldest swimming club in Britain, having celebrated its 150th anniversary in 2014, and hosts the best known group of winter swimmers in the UK. The Serpentine Swimming Club (SSC) held its first Christmas Day Race in 1864. It was then men only and the club's facilities consisted of a bench under an elm tree where members could leave their clothes. Nowadays the club has a basic indoor changing area separate from the public facilities but, if you visit during public opening hours, you will be able to use the Lido's changing rooms, buy coffee and ice-cream at the café and sit on the manicured lawns. The club still organises races every Saturday and its Christmas Day Peter Pan cup is named after JM Barrie, who was a supporter although not a swimmer.

According to the SSC website, women were not able to swim in the Serpentine until the Lido opened on June 16th 1930. On the opening day, throngs of women queued to get entry and the first in, 21-year-old Kathleen Murphy of Pinner, had arrived at 5am.

By the 1960s some women were swimming with the club throughout the year. An early pioneer, police officer Gail Oxley, would race down from a parked squad car, do a quick change out of uniform, sprint through the water, then run back to the car. Luckily an emergency call never caught her out. Alan Titmuss, in his book on the club's history, *Breaking the Ice*, recounts the reaction of one of the older members to Gail's quick change of apparel: his glasses steaming up! Attitudes have since moved on – shared changing for club members no longer seems a problem.

The lake hosted the men's and women's open water swimming and triathlon events in the London 2012 Olympics. You can enjoy the delights of swimming in the Serpentine at a more leisurely

INFORMATION

DISTANCE: 4 miles.
TIME: 2 hours.
MAP: OS Landranger 176 (West London); OS Explorer 173 (London North); London A-Z.
START POINT: Leicester Square Underground Station.
END POINT: Marble Arch Underground Station.
PUBLIC TRANSPORT: Northern or Piccadilly lines to Leicester Square; Central line from Marble Arch; buses.
SWIMMING: The Serpentine Lido and its accompanying paddling pool is open to the public every day in high summer from 10am-6pm and for parts of May and September. There are lifeguards and basic changing facilities and entry is £4.60 adult, £3.60 concessions, £1.60 child. Visit www.royalparks.org.uk or call 020 7706 3422 for full details. Members of the Serpentine Swimming Club swim every day between 6am and 9.30am.
PLACES OF INTEREST: Trafalgar Square; Banqueting House; government buildings in Whitehall; Parliament Square; St James's Palace; the Royal Parks.
REFRESHMENTS: St Martin-in-the-Fields Café in the Crypt (WC2N 5DN, tel 020 7766 1158); Serpentine Bar and Kitchen (W2 2UH, tel 020 7706 8114); Lido Kiosk and Lido Café Bar (W2 2UH, tel 020 7706 7098); Serpentine Gallery Pavilion (summer only, W2 3XA, tel 020 7402 6075); coffee van at Italian Gardens.

pace, or simply soak up the sun and the sky, sheltered from the hustle and bustle of the city beyond by the magnificent trees. Look out for the solar-powered passenger boat, the Solarshuttle, silently criss-crossing the lake.

The lake was created by damming the Westbourne River in the 18th century and was one of the first examples of the English preference for landscaping parks to make them look natural. By then the park had been open to the public for 100 years. Before that it was a hunting reserve, created for Henry VIII. Hyde Park is still owned by the Crown. The Princess Diana Memorial Fountain ❺ is just outside the Lido and a playground dedicated to her is to the west of the lake in Kensington Gardens.

Before reaching the Serpentine, the walk takes us through the compact area where political power over England, Britain and then the British Empire has been exercised for a millennium. The medieval monarchs ruled from their Palace of Westminster, site now of the Houses of Parliament. Henry VIII moved the court and its offices to Whitehall Palace. The royal family later moved to St James's Palace ❸, which is still the address for the official business of the monarchy and home to some family members.

Halfway down Whitehall is one good place to pause. It was outside the white stone Banqueting House ❶, the only surviving part of Whitehall Palace, that Charles I was executed. A temporary platform was built and the king had to step over the sill of a first floor window to go to his death.

A statue of Charles, looking too small for his horse, as in life, is on the roundabout in front of Nelson's Column. His nemesis, Oliver

Cromwell, leader of the Parliamentary forces that defeated Charles, stands at the other end of Whitehall in front of Westminster Hall ❷. This medieval building, now part of the Houses of Parliament, is the only remnant of the original Palace of Westminster.

To balance this tour of power, the walk begins in Trafalgar Square, which has been the scene of public demonstrations since it was built in the early 19th century. The largest ever demonstration, when millions protested against the Iraq War, took place in 2003, and one of the longest lasting was the protest against apartheid outside South Africa House, which ended with the release of Nelson Mandela.

The walk ends at Speakers' Corner ❻. Now mainly deserted – the internet having provided everyone with their own soap box – information boards record how this part of Hyde Park was the site of countless demonstrations before being officially designated as a place where people could speak publicly. Its deeper history lies in its proximity to the site of the gallows at Tyburn, where 50,000 people were executed by the state over six centuries until 1783.

Everywhere along the route you will see memorials to those killed in battle and statues of military leaders, many commemorating wars of the British Empire. Some recent commissions, such as the memorial to the women who served in World War II ❶ and the Memorial Gates ❹ honouring the contribution of Indians, Africans and Caribbeans, give belated recognition to those not previously commemorated.

Quite a slice of history, but the calming water of the Serpentine awaits.

❶ TRAFALGAR SQUARE

Start from Leicester Square Underground Station. Walk down Charing Cross Road and into the centre of Trafalgar Square. The South African Embassy is on the east side, and the National Gallery on the north. Walk round the square, passing Nelson's Column on your left. Cross to the roundabout in front of Nelson's Column. Head down Whitehall towards the tower with Big Ben. Cross to the left side at Horse Guards Avenue to read the information board outside the Banqueting House.
0.5 miles

❷ WHITEHALL AND PARLIAMENT SQUARE

Pass the Ministry of Defence, the Women of World War II Memorial, the Cenotaph and the entrance to Downing Street on the right. At the traffic lights, cross Bridge Street and walk past the Houses of Parliament to the statue of Oliver Cromwell. Retrace your steps. With Westminster Abbey to your left, cross onto the grass in the centre of the square to inspect the statues of key political figures, including Nelson Mandela and Winston Churchill. Cross the road to the left of Abraham Lincoln, and turn left. Turn right in front of Central Hall Westminster, and walk to the end of Storey's Gate. Turn left, then immediately cross the road at the pedestrian crossing and walk ahead on Horse Guards Road. Pass the Cabinet War Rooms on your right and turn left into St James's Park.
1 mile

❸ ST JAMES'S PARK

Follow the path along the south side of St James's Park Lake, round the west end and back along the north side (or take a shortcut across the bridge). When you reach the bridge, turn left, cross the Mall and go ahead into Marlborough Road. Turn left as you follow the wall of St James's Palace. Turn right passing 8 Cleveland Row and Selwyn House. Turn left.
2 miles

❹ HYDE PARK AND THE SERPENTINE

Go through the gated path to join the Queen's Walk. Green Park is ahead of you and Buckingham Palace to your left. Head slightly to the left to see Fallen Leaves, the Canadian War Memorial, then keep going roughly parallel to the road on your left to reach the Memorial Gates. Cross the roundabout and walk through the Wellington Arch, past the Australian and Royal Artillery war memorials. Cross onto the triangular traffic island then in through the gates of Hyde Park. Cross the two lanes of the road within the park, turn left along the side of the sandy horse track then take the path that goes off diagonally right. Walk through the rose garden, exiting at the end to the left then walk ahead and slightly to the right to reach the large natural stones of the Holocaust Memorial Garden. Cross the road and turn right, then left to walk along the south side of the Serpentine Lake. Keep going until you reach the Serpentine Lido.
3 miles

❺ TO LONG WATER

After your swim, continue along the side of the Lake. Just after passing the Princess Diana Memorial Fountain take the left hand fork, cross the road and turn left to the Serpentine Gallery and Pavilion (summer only). From the Gallery strike out across the park to return to the bank of the lake, now officially the Long Water. Follow the lake to the Italian Gardens. Cross at the top and walk back along the north side of the park, picking a route not too close to the busy Bayswater Road.
4 miles

❻ SPEAKERS' CORNER

Keep going until you see the notice boards of Speakers' Corner between the Marble Arch roundabout and Park Lane stretching down to the right. Walk ahead to the tube station.

Ros Bayley, Cath Cinnamon.

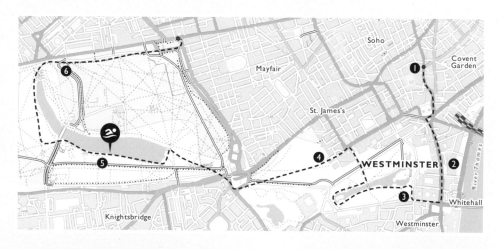

45

Walk 4

FARNHAM TO FRENSHAM GREAT POND OR TO BENTLEY STATION

A varied walk (with shorter and longer options) through woods, meadows and heathland with two contrasting swims.

*T*his walk offers a glorious day out exploring varied landscapes over good terrain with several little gems to discover. It is great for dogs, too, as they will meet friends along the way and are allowed at the Frensham Ponds if they are on leads. The main swim is in Frensham Great Pond ❼, which looks like a natural lake but in fact is artificial, dug out in the Middle Ages as a fishpond for the Bishop of Winchester. There are also swims ❹ in the young River Wey, which feeds the ponds and is small here, only just deep enough to swim in places, yet pretty, clear and surprisingly cold.

On a hot, sunny August day the swim in the Wey was wonderfully refreshing and, although only a short walk from a busy common by Tilford Bridge, it felt quiet and secretive. We entered the water down a steep bank where a fencepost provided a handhold but further on, near a bench, there is an easier entry point although the river is shallower there.

Frensham Great Pond was very different with cheerful crowds enjoying the sandy beach and tepid water. It is a popular place for families and there is a car park and café. The pond is used by a sailing club and swimmers are not supposed to go beyond a little roped-off area which, during dry weather, can be too shallow for comfortable swimming. Some of us slipped under the rope after checking that the boats were far away. Another time in November the beach was deserted and the water deeper and, of course, colder. Despite having few customers the café was open and provided a very welcome hot tea.

There are many points of interest on the walk. Not far from the start there is a strange carved bench ❶ made by local art students, and soon afterwards look out for Billy the alpaca in a field to the

INFORMATION

DISTANCE: 8 miles to Frensham Great Pond; 13 miles to Bentley Station.
TIME: 4.5 hours or 7 hours.
Map OS Landranger 186 (Aldershot and Guildford); OS Explorer 145 (Guildford and Farnham); for the Bentley option only, OS Explorer 144 (Basingstoke).
START POINT: Farnham Station.
END POINT, short route: Bus stop by Frensham Great Pond; long route: Bentley Station.
PUBLIC TRANSPORT: Train from Waterloo to Farnham. From Frensham Great Pond: bus to Farnham Station from nearby stop on A287 (at time of writing an hourly service on bus 19 is operated by Stagecoach but no service on Sundays, see www. stagecoachbus.com); Fox Taxis (tel 01252 856242). From Bentley: train via Farnham to Waterloo.
SWIMMING: In the River Wey and Frensham Great Pond.
PLACES OF INTEREST: Moor Park House; World War II defences; the Wey Valley; Frensham Common.
REFRESHMENTS: The Barley Mow pub, Tilford (GU10 2BU, tel 01252 792205); tea stall at Frensham Great Pond; The Bluebell pub, Dockenfield (GU10 4EX, tel 01252 792801); Café on the Green, Alice Holt Forest Centre (GU10 4LS, tel 01420 520212).

right of the path. Apparently he has a habit of breaking out and turning up unannounced in local gardens, but is always welcomed.

Moor Park House ❷, near where the route leaves the North Downs Way, is not open to the public but displays an information board. Once famed for its gardens, it belonged to Sir William Temple, whose secretary was Jonathan Swift, author of *Gulliver's Travels*. The garden is now turfed over, with a retaining wall. A little further on are the remains of a World War II pillbox ❷, part of the GHQ (General Headquarters) Line, a system of defences built across England to delay German forces in the event of an invasion. There is another pillbox in the valley near the ruined Waverley Abbey, and more in Moor Park. These, and the river's natural defence, were a crucial part of the defence plan.

The path continues through beautiful woods to pass a cave, now with an ornate gated entrance, known as Mother Ludlam's Cave ❷. The story goes that in the Middle Ages the local water supply dried up, then a monk from Waverley Abbey found the spring inside the cave, so the abbey again had an assured supply of water. Mother Ludlam is the subject of another set of legends. The best known

version is that she was a kindly white witch who lived in the cave and lent utensils to poor people, until one day a cauldron was not returned and she flew into a rage. The borrower sought refuge in Frensham church, and the cauldron remains in the church to this day and is believed to have been used for brewing church ale.

The ruins of Waverley Abbey ❸ are barely visible through the trees in summer. They can be reached by making a small detour but are worth a longer visit than there may be time for on this walk.

Just past Tilford, and near to where we swam, the Wey runs through well maintained woodland. Along the banks here we came across two rangers picking Himalayan balsam. They told us that the invasive species had quite taken over the waterway but that systematic picking had almost eradicated it. Another passer-by told us he had just seen a kingfisher.

The longer route beyond Frensham Pond to Bentley passes through fields and beautiful woodland surrounding Alice Holt Lodge, a Forestry Commission research station. On a warm June day there were foxgloves and orchids, skylarks singing and several kinds of butterflies.

DIRECTIONS

❶ **FROM FARNHAM STATION**
Exit from Platform 1. Ahead of you is Station Hill, heading down to the busy A31. At the corner with the A31 dual carriageway there is a hard-to-spot waymark for the North Downs Way. Turn

right along the A31 and very soon turn off it right on a lane signposted North Downs Way. The lane soon runs beside the River Wey on the left, with some attractive houses on the right. After less than half a mile

it bears right under the railway and continues with woods on the right and the valley floor on the left. Ignore a couple of paths heading uphill right but just before the track enters an open meadow turn off it to the right,

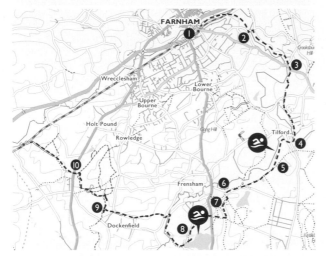

still following the North Downs Way, through a little gate by a carved seat. When the path reaches a minor road follow the road left and continue as it bears left again after about 100 metres, with a sign indicating Surrey Cycleway Link.
1.25 miles

❷ MOOR PARK HOUSE
Cross the river and walk past the new-build complex on the right hand side to reach Moor Park House. Opposite a cycle track on the left take a FP to the right, leaving the North Downs Way, to go through a little metal gate beside bigger

gates onto a driveway past Moor Park House. The driveway turns into a path, passes remains of World War II defences and continues through woods past Mother Ludlam's Cave.
2.25 miles

❸ TOWARDS TILFORD
On reaching a road turn right and almost immediately left at a road junction. After about 150 metres turn right onto a byway, which goes gently downhill through woods. After about quarter of a mile follow the byway to the right, ignoring a path straight on. On reaching a minor road cross and continue on a signposted track the other side. Be careful to avoid a house drive by following waymarks along a narrow, fenced track with a house on the right and a farm building housing a garage on the left. The track becomes a shady lane and soon goes slightly downhill through a tunnel of holly trees, becomes a tarmac lane with houses (under construction when we visited) on the left and turns left just past the houses. Do not follow it left but take a bridleway slightly to the right and parallel to the Wey. This joins a road at Tilford near a bridge and small weir where the bank on the far side is a popular picnic spot and paddling place.
4 miles

❹ TILFORD GREEN
Turn right to cross the bridge and follow the road straight on passing a large green on the left

and the Barley Mow pub on the right. On reaching a somewhat complex junction, head across the road to the entrance of a plant nursery and take a well concealed FP that runs to the left of a house and the right of the nursery (behind conifers). After about 100 metres you can reconnect with the river and a smaller path on the bank where you can choose a spot to swim.
4.25 miles

❺ TO PRIORY LANE
The path continues by the river, then veers away and comes out onto a tarmac track. Keep right here and continue as the track gradually turns into a dirt track which passes some houses on the right, goes through a metal gate and becomes a path with wire both sides. When we walked it there were pigs in the pens on both sides. There is a boardwalk because the path becomes swampy in bad weather. Where the track joins a bigger, sandy lane, turn right onto it and continue through mixed wood, pine and bracken to reach a very minor road, Priory Lane.
5.5 miles

❻ FRENSHAM LITTLE POND
Turn left on the road and after a few paces take a path to the right. Follow this until you see ahead a small building and a paddock. Then veer right to go up a small rise from where you will see Little Frensham Pond to the left. Walk along the bank

keeping the pond on the left but when the bank veers left keep to the track, which goes straight on and uphill across open heathland (which, when we walked it showed signs of fire and of new planting with birch). At the top of the hill there is a bench; if you stand on it you can just see Frensham Great Pond.
6.5 miles

❼ FRENSHAM COMMON
Turn left on a sandy track and take the first waymarked track on the right downhill towards the main A287 road between you and Frensham Great Pond. Before reaching the road take a waymarked path left which eventually leads you onto the road by bus stops. Cross the road and find a sandy path between areas of fenced ground to arrive at Frensham Great Pond. Follow the bank for about 50 metres to a beach. Visible, away to the right, is a wooden block with a café and also a car park.
8 miles

For the short route: after swimming return to the road to catch a bus. For the longer route:
❽ TO DOCKENFIELD AND BATT'S CORNER
After swimming follow a path round the pond to the right with the pond on the left. When the path joins a road bear left to continue in the same general direction. At a bend take a signed path to the right through a wooded valley beside a

stream, which widens into a pool, contracts into a stream again and joins the River Wey. Ignore a bridge on your left and continue to a road. Turn left to cross the Wey, turn left again at a road junction and then take a FP on the right just before a house. After about three quarters of a mile, a house (Orchard End) comes into view. Continue in the same general direction on varying track surfaces through the scattered houses of Dockenfield, bearing left at Keeper's Cottage, to reach a T-junction at Batt's Corner just after the Bluebell pub. Turn left to another T-junction where you turn right towards Bucks Horn Oak.
10.5 miles

❾ ON SHIPWRIGHTS WAY
Soon after the T-junction take a bridleway to the right, opposite Abbotswood Lodge and signed Shipwrights Way. It wanders through the woods to the Alice Holt Forest Centre and then on to the main A325.
11.5 miles

❿ PAST ALICE HOLT LODGE.
Cross with care and continue on the Shipwrights Way. After about a third of a mile, you pass the Forestry Commission's Alice Holt Lodge on your right. Continue on the tarmac track to reach the station.
13 miles

Margaret Dickinson, Sally Davey and Tim Loonen, Liz Valentine.

Walk 5

RICKMANSWORTH CIRCULAR

A gentle walk easily reached from London yet with a truly rural feel. Enjoy a swim in the River Colne and possibly Bury Lake.

INFORMATION

DISTANCE: 6 miles.
TIME: 3 hours.
Map Landranger 176 (West London); OS Explorer 172 (Chiltern Hills East).
START POINT: Rickmansworth Underground Station.
END POINT: Rickmansworth Underground Station.
PUBLIC TRANSPORT: Metropolitan line or Chiltern Railways from Marylebone (shorter journey time but less frequent service).
PLACES OF INTEREST: Rickmansworth village; Stocker's Lake Nature Reserve (WD3 1NB, tel 01727 858901).
SWIMMING: In Bury Lake if it becomes permitted, otherwise a dip in the River Colne.
REFRESHMENTS: Plenty of pubs, cafés and restaurants in Rickmansworth, including The Oaks gastropub, West Hyde (WD3 9XP, tel 01895 822118).

Although this walk is within the M25, much of it feels like deep countryside. The highlight is the string of great lakes that run along the Colne Valley. They are flooded gravel pits, dug out originally to supply the construction industry building an ever-expanding London. The gravel was deposited by an ancient river, ancestor of our Thames, which – before the Ice Age – flowed up the Colne Valley on its way to join the Rhine.

The starting point, Rickmansworth ❶, is built at the confluence of three rivers: the Gade, the Colne and the Chess, and contains a few medieval houses amidst indifferent modern development. The route passes St Mary's church ❷, an attractive building although not as old as it looks. Nearby Stocker's Lake is home to many waterfowl, especially during the winter months. Walking the route in mid-September, we saw house martins and great crested grebes, beautiful red guelder rose leaves and berries, and feasted on many sweet blackberries along the way.

Putting this walk in the Ponds section of this book is a gesture of optimism because the ideal swimming place would be Bury Lake ❸ where, at the time of writing, the right to swim is contested. It was a popular swimming place until the late 1980s (indeed one of us has still vivid memories dating back over 50 years of an idyllic day spent relaxing there after A level exams). Then the Three Rivers District Council banned swimming on the grounds that there were health and safety issues to do with occasional algae blooms, deep water and possible risks owing to shared use with a sailing club. Since 2006 there has been a vigorous campaign to get the ban removed. KLPA member Molly Fletcher has played a leading part in this, and when members of the River and Lake Swimming Association handed a 700-signature petition to the Three Rivers District Council demanding they be allowed back in the water there was a moment of apparent success when 'No swimming' signs were removed. Later, however, the council decided to uphold the ban, and the sailing club that uses the lake remained opposed to reinstating swimming. When we were there in 2013 the situation was

unclear. We did not see a 'No swimming' sign, but there was no barrier separating a swimming area from boats as there used to be in the days when it was a recognised bathing spot.

Bury is one of 25 lakes in the Colne Valley and it seems so sad that not one of them is for swimming. We hope that reason will prevail and people will again be allowed to swim at their own risk in this lovely stretch of water.

DIRECTIONS

❶ RICKMANSWORTH
Turn right out of the station and then right underneath the railway and downhill to a main shopping street, High Street, where you turn left. Continue along, then turn right at the crossroads into Church Street, down to St Mary's church.

❷ ST MARY'S CHURCH
Go through the churchyard, cross the road and turn right to a roundabout, which you go round to the left towards a bridge carrying the main road over the Grand Union Canal. From the bridge, just before a zebra crossing, take steps on the left down to the canal towpath. Go under the bridge, continuing in a westerly direction. You soon see a large Tesco on the other side of the canal on your left. Here, just after a bridge over a side stream, go slightly to the right and then left to follow a track

(signed Batchworth Lake Circular Walk) parallel to the canal and beside a lake which leads you round and then towards a car park. Bypass the car park by veering left and you come to a second stretch of water, Bury Lake, the focus of the campaign to restore public swimming.

❸ BURY LAKE
Go along the south side of the lake on a narrow, slightly overgrown path. At the far end you see a building which is the sailing club. Walk past it then turn right onto the FP between Bury Lake on your right and Stocker's Lake on your left. Follow this path until you reach the River Colne, then take a path to the left (signed to Springwell and Inn Lakes) alongside the river, with Stocker's Lake on your left.
1 mile

❹ RIVER COLNE
This is the place where a dip in the Colne is possible. The river is fast flowing and quite shallow with a firm bottom. Further along, it becomes deeper and slower but lacks a safe entry point as the banks drop steeply down, and the bottom is soft and muddy. Further down there is a place below a weir that might be suitable but, being close to a car park, it is rather public. Refreshed from your swim, continue along the path beside the River Colne, bearing right with the river after the weir, until you reach a road (opposite Willow Court).

❺ FOLLOW THE CANAL
Turn left and walk down the road to meet the canal. Turn right along it for a short distance then go left over the bridge at Springwell Lock, joining the Hillingdon Trail (HT).

DIRECTIONS

⑥ HILLINGDON TRAIL

Turn right over the bridge onto a little road. Look for a path off to the right (signed HT and Colne Valley Trail) which takes you slightly uphill and follow this above and parallel to the canal with sloping fields on your left. Ignore the left turn uphill (on HT), instead keeping straight ahead on the Colne Valley Trail, with the sewage works away to the right, until you come down to the waterside near West Hyde.
3.5 miles

⑦ WEST HYDE

Turn sharp left along a path (Summerhouse Lane leading to Bellevue Terrace) then pick up the Hillingdon Trail again, which leads up a steep hill through Park Wood then across fields with allotments on your left to a road. Turn left here for a short distance then first right into Plough Lane, following the London Loop signs. This leads over a stile into a field. Follow the path through several fields, eventually joining a track which takes you out to the busy Harefield Road.
4.5 miles

⑧ APPROACHING RICKMANSWORTH

Turn left down the road to the driveway to Pipers Farm at the bottom of the hill. Here you will find a footpath on the right that starts just by the driveway and runs roughly parallel to the road. It climbs up through some trees then along the edge of a golf course before gradually dropping

down to a minor road. Follow this to the right, then veer left and either continue or take a short footpath to a road where you turn right. The road passes Tesco on your left and soon joins the big main road by the roundabout near St Mary's church. Retrace your steps to Rickmansworth tube.
6 miles

Margaret Dickinson, Liz Valentine

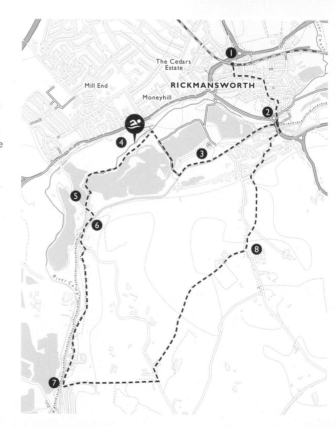

Rivers

London and its surrounding countryside are crossed by many rivers and each offers a series of potential swimming spots along its course.

So, in this section our difficulty has been narrowing our choice. The Thames dominates, not only because it has shaped our capital and history, but also it is a surprisingly clean river for its size, it has enshrined access rights, and it is reliably deep but with plenty of beach sections. The five Thames walks share a river but otherwise vary in length and character, with a town route through Oxford and four rural walks. These range from the more strenuous Marlow Circulars, which cross some hilly country above the river, to Goring-to-Cholsey, an easy riverside wander that's ideal for a hot day when it is good to have time for many swims.

For the other walks, we include only one per river – although the Wey sneaks in an extra appearance in the Farnham to Frensham Great Pond walk – and we do not have space to cover all the good swimming rivers in the region; you might also like to try the Ouse (Sussex), the Stour (Kent) and the Great Ouse (Bedfordshire). We selected the walks partly according to their ease of access, and partly for a reasonable balance between north, east and south, given that the Thames walks are all to the west.

Each river has its individual character, but a common feature of those included is that, once they are deep enough to swim in, they tend to be fairly slow moving and cloudy, flowing over gravelly, sandy or muddy beds. The reason is that the region rests on soft rocks like clays, chalk and sandstones, which are relatively easily eroded. It lacks outcrops of ancient hard rock like granite that resist erosion, so you won't find the natural waterfalls and clear rockpools of the West Country, Wales or the North.

Instead there are spectacular man-made weir pools, and you will often find some wonderful deep natural pools with beaches, particularly at meanders (beach on the inside, deep on the out). Remember never to play on or under the Thames weirs – they are far too powerful with dangerous undercurrents – and never to swim after heavy rain when the river is swollen, because of poor water quality as well as fast flow.

Walk 6

WATTON-AT-STONE TO HERTFORD, HERTFORDSHIRE

This gently rural walk follows the River Beane through different phases of its life, from rushing stream, to reedy pools, to the deep meanders of the final swimming place.

INFORMATION

DISTANCE: 8 miles.
TIME: 4 hours.
MAP: OS Landranger 166 (Luton & Hertford) or OS Explorer 194 (Hertford & Bishop Stortford).
START POINT: Watton-at-Stone Station.
END POINT: Hertford North Station.
PUBLIC TRANSPORT: Train from King's Cross (weekends) or Moorgate (weekdays). Return from Hertford North; also possible from Hertford East but check whether your day return is valid on that line.
SWIMMING: In the River Beane, at least two possible places.
PLACES OF INTEREST: Woodhall Park; Lee Navigation; Waterford Heath Nature Park; St Leonard's church, Bengeo; Hertford historic town.
REFRESHMENTS: Two pubs in Watton-at-Stone, The Bull (tel 01920 831032) and The George and Dragon (01920 830285), both in the High Street. The Woodhall Arms, Stapleford (SG14 3NW, tel 01992 535123). Hertford pubs and cafés including an open-air tea place near the end of the walk.

The Hertfordshire landscape exudes moderation. There are little woods, pocket-sized nature reserves and gentle undulations instead of hills. Even commercial monoculture and suburban sprawl, except around the biggest towns, occur as modest interruptions to the traditional rural scenery. The Beane, appropriately, is a river in miniature. It rises only a few miles above Watton-at-Stone and ends its life near our last swimming place when it joins the Lea. Yet in that short distance it matures and ages like the great rivers of the world, starting fast, shallow and fairly straight, becoming slower and deeper and more curvaceous, until it runs really deep and meandering over a flood plain to join the Lea, or more correctly the Lee, Navigation.

The natural sequence is partly obscured by centuries of human intervention. Water extraction from the catchment area recently caused part of the upper Beane to disappear. At Watton-at-Stone, a flow that once powered a large mill is now reduced to a trickle. The walk joins the Beane where it has been dammed to create water features for Woodhall Park, the neo-classical building which dominates the view as you approach. The lake, weir and weir pool there ❷ date from 1775 when the present house was built.

Downstream from Woodhall Park the river reverts to a young stream rushing over stony shallows – no use for swimming, but the walk beside it is delightful ❸. We passed drifts of speedwell and watched a family of ducks play out a little drama as two dawdlers from the brood let out poignant distress calls and the mother duck struggled against the current to retrieve them.

The river runs on fast and shallow past the tiny village of Stapleford ❸ and its church, St Mary the Virgin (a key is obtainable from a nearby house, and the Norman north door is worth a look). About a mile further on, near Waterford, where the land flattens out and the river starts to slow, there are more signs of human intervention as the area ❹ was used for sand and gravel extraction until the 1990s, with quarrying to the north and settling beds to the south. After the works closed, Waterford Heath became a nature reserve noted for Grizzled Skipper butterflies, which feed on abundant wild strawberries, and according to the information board, is home to great horsetail, orchids, kingfishers and water vole.

In June there were lots of wild flowers including viper's bugloss, mallow and rosebay willow herb. Over the course of the walk we saw many species of butterfly including Marbled White, the beautiful velvety Ringlet, Small Tortoiseshell, Red Admiral, Small Skipper, Small White and Common Blue, as well as Banded Demoiselle damselflies. We heard garden warbler, blackcap, whitethroat and robin singing and saw a tree creeper.

Beyond Waterford Heath, Waterford Marshes ❺ is a pleasant area of wet meadow where the Beane at first runs wide and shallow – good for paddling – then passes through reed beds and becomes deep enough to swim, mostly about waist deep and still quite narrow. There is a distinct current here and the edge is a little muddy, but once away from the bank the bottom is firm and gravelly. At one point there is a convenient bench. Our swim was slightly marred by a herd of bullocks, which arrived just as we were getting out. Two of them started experimentally nibbling our clothes and the largest beast leant forward and prodded one of us on the bottom with his nose, as if to tip us amusingly back into the water. Despite their sweet breath and innocent eyes we were glad to get away.

After Waterford the walk leaves the river to take a shortcut across a bend and rejoins it by Hartham Meadow. It passes St Leonard's, one of only three churches in the county with an apse and 'a rare example of a virtually intact Norman village church' according to Pevsner (the 46-volume series of county-by-county architectural guides, *The Buildings of England*, by Sir Nikolaus Bernhard Leon Pevsner). You then descend to the river as it meanders across a flood plain to debouch into the Lee Navigation. This is where the best swims of the walk are ❽, although they're only suitable for those happy to swim out of their depth. The river here is deep, fairly wide with a good stretch offering reasonably easy entry points. One drawback is that the area is so close to Hertford and Ware that it is busy with people and dogs on fine weekends.

The walk turns back to Hertford along the Lee Navigation, a waterway created by improving the River Lea in order to ship goods in and out of London. It has a special place in canal history because the Act of Parliament for improving the river was passed in 1425 and is the first Act for navigational improvement of any river.

DIRECTIONS

❶ WATTON-AT-STONE

Turn left out of the station along a road with a new housing development on the right. Just after this take a little cul-de-sac on the right, Glebe Close. At the end, take a FP on the left and almost immediately turn right on an enclosed path, which soon reaches a minor road (Church Lane). Turn left and by the church (St Andrew and St Mary) turn right into Perrywood Lane. After about 100 metres, just after a house, take a track left between metal posts. After passing a yard on the left, it becomes a grassy path. After sheds on the left, enter Woodhall Park Estate and take the left fork through two fields with distant views of Woodhall Park house. On reaching the busy A119, cross and take a driveway opposite, indicated by a footpath sign.
1.25 miles

❷ FIRST SIGHT OF THE RIVER BEANE

You reach the River Beane where a weir has created a lake upstream and a weir pool downstream. Continue to cross a stone bridge over the Beane then turn right to pass between the river on the right and Home Farm buildings on the left. After the buildings the track veers left.

At the next junction turn right on a track over a stone bridge. Here we join the Hertfordshire Way (HW), which we follow to the outskirts of Hertford. After crossing a second bridge, look out for a kissing gate in a metal fence, to the right. The path heads diagonally across a field with the river away on the right. (This stretch might be swimmable, but soon there is a weir after which the river becomes fast and shallow).
1.75 miles

❸ TO STAPLEFORD

The path goes to a stone wall, which you cross by a ladder stile. Continue beside the river, ignoring a cross path, to the hamlet of Stapleford, where the path comes out on a residential road. At the junction with a minor road, turn right and then left on a path by the church (St Mary the Virgin).
2.5 miles

❹ TO WATERFORD HEATH

The path hugs the river until, after about half a mile, it veers away, goes slightly uphill and turns right on a farm track to join a road at a right angle bend. Go straight on to a road T-junction. Turn left and after a few yards take a footpath to the right across Waterford

Heath and under the railway to emerge on a road in a small housing estate.
3.75 miles

❺ WATERFORD MARSHES

Continue along the road to a junction. Turn right and almost at once take the HW footpath on the left across Waterford Marshes, where there are possible swimming places. The path eventually leads to the main A119 road.
4.5 miles

❻ ENTERING HERTFORD

Turn left on the A119 and walk along it to a little bridge over a water channel and just afterwards take a path to the left along the edge of the channel.

❼ TO ST LEONARD'S

Continue under the railway. At the next junction, where you meet a metalled surface (there is a bridge to a private road on the left), continue straight on past Molewood House (on the right), between steep, wooded banks on the left and the River Beane close beside you on the right. After about a quarter of a mile, as the houses on Molewood Road appear, take a sharp left turn on a path uphill with steps, leaving the

HW. Pass Fanshawe Street on the right. At the top, continue along Church Road, passing Elton Road on the right. At the T-junction at the end of Church Road, turn right into Duncombe Road, pass Cross Road on the left and where Duncombe Road becomes Farquhar Street, opposite Byde Street, take a footpath on the left between walls. On reaching Bengeo Street, cross over and turn right downhill. Towards the bottom take a path left, signed for the Norman church of St Leonard, with steep wooded banks on your left. Soon our old friend, the river Beane, reappears. Pass a footbridge and tennis courts on the right. A section of the HW comes in from the right. Next there is Hartham Grazing Meadows information board. Continue uphill to St Leonard's church and past it, signed HW, Ware Park Road and Hertford Lock, also Old Bengeo House. To the east of the church, pass through a wooden kissing gate into a meadow. Descend to a footbridge over the River Beane, where both upriver and downriver there are good swimming spots.
6.25 miles

❽ THE LEE NAVIGATION

From the footbridge take the path straight on across the meadow to a bridge over the Lee Navigation at Hertford Lock. Cross and turn right along the towpath, signed to Hertford. At the first bridge over the Lee do not take a path off left signed to the centre of town but at the next bridge your path leaves the waterside. Follow it up left; turn right over the Lee and then left over another waterway. To explore the centre of Hertford, turn left on a long bridge above a weir following signs to the town centre or castle. To go directly to the station, turn right down some steps, cross another bridge and turn left on a path signed to the Leisure Centre, passing the long weir on your left. The path passes Hartham Leisure Centre, a play area and tea stall and goes under a bridge to come out on a grassy area near a big Sainsbury's.
7 miles

❾ TO HERTFORD NORTH STATION

Leaving Sainsbury's to your left, take Port Hill road to cross the Beane. At the junction with another section of Port Hill turn left and soon turn right onto Port Vale. Just after Beane River View and before the Two Brewers and George Street on the right, turn left into a car park to reach an enclosed footpath, which later bears right. Follow it with the river on your left until you reach Beane Road. Turn left for the station.
8 miles

Margaret Dickinson, Liz Valentine.

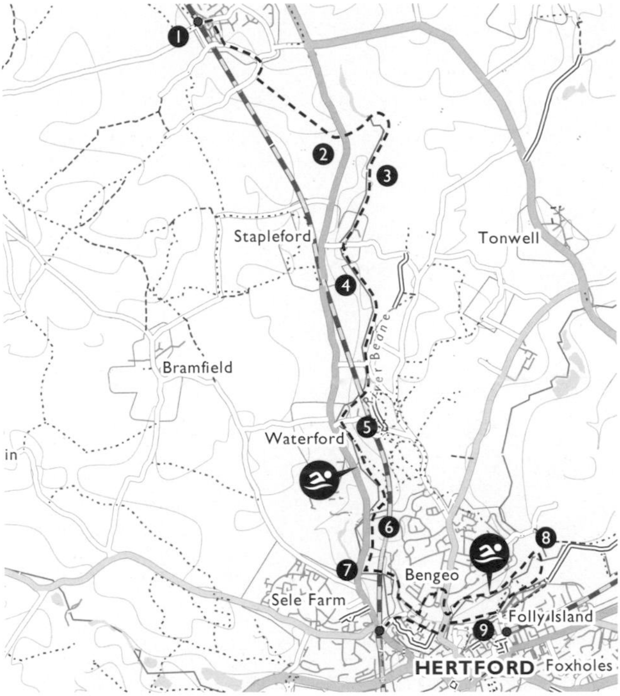

Walk 7

SHEPRETH TO CAMBRIDGE, CAMBRIDGESHIRE

A moderately long walk across stretches of East Anglian farmland, passing through several attractive villages with traditional thatched cottages, via Grantchester to Cambridge.

This is a very pleasant outing in spring or early autumn with scope for short or long swims and an extended picnic on the open meadows ⑩ near the historic village of Grantchester. Expect crowds on the river in high summer, especially at weekends, and biting winds in late autumn or winter. The walk can also be combined with punting, useful to accommodate a party including people averse to a long walk. The end of this route passes Scudamore's boat station ⑬ᵇ above the weir below Silver Street Bridge, the traditional location for hiring a punt to go to Grantchester. A punting group could stay on the train to Cambridge, walk from the railway station to Scudamore's, collect a punt and rendezvous with the walkers at Grantchester.

Not surprisingly for a charming village very near to Cambridge, Grantchester can claim an unusual number of famous residents, past and present, many of whom enjoy, or enjoyed, swimming in the Cam. Rupert Brooke spent his days here studying literature, swimming naked and commuting into Cambridge by canoe. Virginia Woolf and EM Forster, philosophers Betrand Russell and Ludwig Wittgenstein, economist John Maynard Keynes and artist Augustus John all joined him, and were keen swimmers too, forming the neo-Pagan contingent of the emerging Bloomsbury Group.

Byron's Pool, under a weir just upstream, was supposedly the poet's favourite swimming spot and his ghost is invoked by Rupert Brooke in the poem *The Old Vicarage, Grantchester*, written when Brooke was in Germany, nostalgic for life in Cambridge:

INFORMATION

DISTANCE: 9.5 miles.
TIME: 4 to 5 hours.
MAPS: OS Landranger 154 (Cambridge & Newmarket) or OS Explorer 209 (Cambridge).
START POINT: Shepreth Station.
END POINT: Cambridge Station.
PUBLIC TRANSPORT: By train from King's Cross or Finsbury Park. Purchase a day return ticket to Cambridge but take care to catch the stopping train on the outward journey.
SWIMMING: In the River Cam (or Granta, to use the archaic name), a clear river with a modest current.
PLACES OF INTEREST: Barrington church; Haslingfield church; the Mullard Radio Astronomy Observatory; Grantchester riverside village; Cambridge colleges, museums and Botanic Garden.
REFRESHMENTS: Village shops in Barrington and Haslingfield; The Red Lion gastropub (CB3 9NF, tel 01223 840121) and the Orchard Tea Gardens (CB3 9N,D tel 01223 551125) in Grantchester.

'...The stream mysterious glides beneath,
Green as a dream and deep as death.
– Oh damn! I know it! and I know
How the May fields all golden show,
And when the day is young and sweet,
Gild gloriously the bare feet
That run to bathe . . .
Du lieber Gott!
Here am I, sweating, sick, and hot,
And there the shadowed waters fresh
Lean up to embrace the naked flesh...'

Today the flesh is less likely to be naked, except perhaps by moonlight or at dawn, and Byron's Pool is too close to the M11, and too blighted by its new concrete weir, to feel in any way romantic. But there are better places to linger further along, and the river offers scope to do a long swim downstream from Grantchester all the way to Newnham, if you have companions to carry bags.

The water is often deep enough to dive into but take care to check.

Only the fastest of walkers could expect to combine the walk with serious sightseeing but it is worth pausing at Barrington church ❸ and Haslingfield church ❺, both fine medieval buildings, and noting in the distance the Mullard Radio Astronomy Observatory ❻. At the end of the walk there is the option of going into Cambridge ⓫ₐ where there is, of course, plenty to explore. The Fitzwilliam Museum closes at 5pm but is free so worth popping into, even for half an hour. Choral evensong in King's College chapel is at 5.30pm Monday to Saturday, but whatever the time it can be pleasant just to wander round the college area. The University Botanic Gardens are on the direct route to the station ⓬ₐ and from April to September are open until 6pm (4.30 or 5pm the rest of the year), but there is an entry charge.

DIRECTIONS

❶ SHEPRETH
Turn left as you get off the train and follow the platform out of Shepreth station. Turn left over the tracks of the level crossing and towards the village taking exceptional care (if the gates are still down another train is coming). Walk past the village hall and the old telephone box (now home to the Shepreth Book Exchange).

Cross the bridge over the stream but veer to the left following a sign for the footpath to Barrington.

❷ TO BARRINGTON
Continue down this side street until it runs out at the railway line. Cross over the gated level crossing with care. Follow the public footpath along the side of two fields. Halfway along the second

field, where a line of telegraph poles marches diagonally across the field, veer to your right, a signed footpath following the line of the poles. Turn left at the other side of the field and go around the field edge, ignoring the bridge on your right over a drainage channel. Cross a newly made marked footbridge on the right over a channel, and shortly afterwards a metal bridge painted green over the main sluice. Continue up the alley between a high yew hedge on the left and high beech hedge on the right to Boot Lane and towards the thatched roofs at the top. This brings you to Barrington village high street and the shop. Turn right out of Boot Lane into the high street and go past the soccer field towards the church.

1.5 miles

❸ BARRINGTON TO HARSTON

Take a right turn at the crossroads just before the church into Challis Green. Follow the road round the playground to a disused phone box. Turn left into Glebe Road and continue past the end of the village, picking up the footpath to Harston across the fields.

❹ Cross the disused railway spur that used to serve the cement works, following the path to a farm building, with two large fuel tanks outside it, where the path veers off to the right (the sign for this is bent but still visible), running along the dyke and round a field beside a narrow sluice drain. The path takes an abrupt right turn over a small footbridge and through a small kissing gate, through the tunnel cut in this hedgerow, between two hedges through another kissing gate, and past a paddock beside a long line of old, large chestnut trees.

3 miles

❺ TO HASLINGFIELD

Turn right at the road, cross the river bridge, and take the first left

beside the church on the western edge of Harston village. Turn immediately left in front of the sign for Church Street and the white cottages, following the sign for a footpath to Haslingfield. Follow this road (Button End) to the dead end. Here the footpath goes across the field beside a hedge, joining a bridleway where you turn left at a T-junction. Cross the stream and follow the path, ignoring a large gate on the right signposted to the Trumpington Estate. At a fork in the path, take the right hand fork. At the bungalows on the edge of Haslingfield, turn left for the shop and church, or turn right past the bungalows for the route to Grantchester.

4 miles

❻ FIELDS WITH VIEWS

Pass a field on the left after the houses containing chicken coops. The path continues straight between fields, giving a view of the chimney and blocky buildings of Addenbrooke's Hospital on the far horizon to the right (on the edge of Cambridge) and on the left a line of radio telescope saucers. Beside an outbuilding with another large black oil tank the path divides again. Veer left here. Ignore the right-hand fork.

5 miles

❼ OVER THE M11

At a large electronic farm gate with a sign to Cantelupe Farm the track surface changes to concrete. Continue straight on, noticing a sign for Grantchester a mile and a half further on. Continue straight up the

public bridleway over the wooden bridge and up the path that runs through the patch of woodland on the other side. Watch out for cyclists here. As you leave this woodland the path forks.

❽ Go right here, round the field edge and up over the raised footbridge across the motorway. The motorway noise disappears remarkably quickly as you leave the bridge behind you and cross the next field. At a three-way turn, take the right-hand path, leaving the church on your left. At the back of the farmyard with a 'No entry' sign, follow the path to the left of the laurel hedge. At the road a large orchard is largely hidden behind the high brick and flint wall directly opposite.

6.75 miles

❾ GRANTCHESTER.

To visit Grantchester church and the pub turn left. To find the Orchard Tea Gardens turn right. To swim and continue the walk turn left, then right at the first bend, down the lane/public footpath towards the river. There are a couple of kissing gates and small fields before the path reaches the riverbank proper.

7 miles

❿ BESIDE THE CAM. You now enter Grantchester Meadows from the village end. At this location the water may not look inviting, and there is little by way of vegetation where you might hide a bag. About 200 metres on, however, there are some large pools with ropes on the opposite bank. This stretch is an ideal place to get into the river. Alternatively, half a mile from Grantchester, there are places with good cover for changing.

⓫ As you get closer towards Cambridge, the path along the bank merges at a narrow point with the paved bike path, after a kissing gate. The last meadow before this is a good place to swim at any time of year.
8.5 miles

⓬ **LEAVING AND REJOINING THE CAM**
As you start walking through Newnham village (on a street still called Grantchester Meadows) veer to the right, leaving a small repair garage (GP Motors) on the left. Turn right at the end of this street, and follow the posts marked with red rings. This will bring you into the Paradise Nature Reserve. Follow the footpath on through the trees here to regain the riverbank.

⓭ **CAMBRIDGE**
Beside a large municipal paddling pool and public toilets, cross the tubular bridge over the river, but pause here because you have a choice.
9.5 miles

⓭ₐ **TO THE STATION**
Continue on the right-hand path over a second bridge, along the edge of Sheep's Green and behind the Leys School along the path beside Vicar's Brook until the Trumpington Road. Turn left and then almost immediately right into Bateman Street. You can opt here

to visit the 40-acre Cambridge University Botanic Garden. Alternatively, continue along Bateman Street. At Hills Road cross straight over and turn right, take the first exit left at the roundabout, Station Road, and follow it to the station.

⓭♭ **INTO CAMBRIDGE**
Turn left immediately after the tubular bridge and follow the path beside the culvert to Fen Causeway. Cross on the diagonal pedestrian crossing and continue to the Mill Pond. Turn right but then take the left fork immediately after this to head diagonally toward the main river. Turn left

along the bank (opposite the large hotel) and walk until you reach Scudamore's boat station and the weir below Silver Street Bridge. From here Mill Lane leads towards the centre of town. Alternatively, to walk along The Backs (a scenic walk behind King's, Trinity and St John's), turn left after the footbridge over the weir at Scudamore's and head up the alley beside the University Sports and Social Club (and bike hire place) to Silver Street. Turn left over Silver Street Bridge and right after 100 metres to pick up the footpath that runs along The Backs.

Hannah Pearce, Liz Valentine

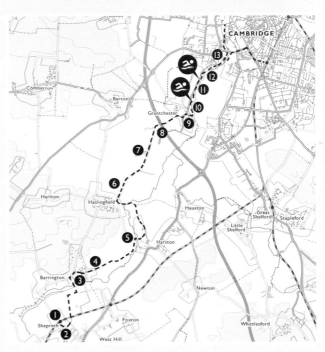

71

HATFIELD PEVEREL CIRCULAR, ESSEX

A short train ride from London, this peaceful rural walk through ancient Essex countryside offers several swims in the clear waters of the Chelmer.

INFORMATION

DISTANCE: 11 miles with a shorter option of 8 miles.
TIME: 5 to 6 hours.
MAP: OS Landranger 167 (Chelmsford) and 168 (Colchester); OS Explorer 183 (Chelmsford & The Rodings).
START AND END POINT: Hatfield Peverel station.
PUBLIC TRANSPORT: Train from Liverpool Street or Stratford.
PLACES OF INTEREST: The Chelmer Navigation; Paper Mill Lock; St Mary the Virgin, Little Baddow; Little Baddow Hall; Little Baddow United Reformed Church; Hoe Mill Lock.
SWIMMING: River Chelmer.
REFRESHMENTS: The Swan Inn, Hatfield Peverel (CM3 2DW, tel 01245 380238); The Stables Tea Room at Paper Mill Lock (CM3 4BS, tel 01245 225520).

The main attractions of this walk are gentle, rural landscapes and the River Chelmer with its dark, clear waters and reed-fringed banks. The river above Paper Mill Lock ❹ is heavily used by canal boats and does not look suitable for swimming, but downstream there are many opportunities to enjoy water that is clean and quite deep with only the gentlest of flow, although access may be a bit muddy. For over a mile the route follows the river and this section provides a perfect opportunity for a long, linear swim if someone is willing to carry your clothes or if the day is warm enough to walk back upstream to collect them.

The Chelmer & Blackwater Navigation was built to link Chelmsford with the Blackwater estuary at Heybridge near Maldon. It was proposed as far back as the 17th century, but opposed by the people of Maldon who feared a loss of trade if boats could carry on to Chelmsford. Work eventually started in the late 18th century and it was eventually opened in 1797.

We first did the walk in October when few of us wanted to swim, and there was some concern about the interest of the walk for non-swimmers. We need not have worried – everyone was pleasantly surprised by the deeply rural feel of the area and the richness of vegetation. Early on we passed a thick hedgerow of hawthorn and spindleberry. In some fields farmers had planted wild flowers and in one place we passed bands of viper's bugloss, flax, mustard, and rat's tail radish, while further on we saw pale pink mallow, evening primroses and the remnants of thistles. Walking the route again in April we heard and saw many birds, including a nightingale and a willow warbler, whitethroats,

swallows and shelduck, and chanced upon hares chasing each other in the fields.

The Chelmer is first reached at a place where there have been mills for hundreds of years, but the name Paper Mill Bridge commemorates the first paper mill in Essex, opened in the 1750s. This is the point where it is possible to shorten the walk by turning downstream, but it is worth first visiting Paper Mill Lock and the Stables café, which sells wonderful cakes.

The full route makes for a better walk, with additional places of interest and lovely views across the valley. It passes the church and manor of Little Baddow, now about a mile away from the modern settlement. The church of St Mary the Virgin apparently has medieval wall paintings, but it was locked when we passed. Roughly opposite the church is Little Baddow Hall, a fine half-timbered, pink-washed building dating from the 14th century. Nearby is Little Baddow United Reformed Church, built in 1708 and one of the earliest Nonconformist chapels in East Anglia. The village was a centre of Puritanism and is associated with two famous preachers, Thomas Hooker and John Eliot.

In the chapel grounds there is a local history centre (open Tuesdays and Thursdays 10am to 12pm and Wednesdays and Sundays 2pm to 4pm).

The patches of woodland around Little Baddow are remnants of the great forest which once covered most of Essex. Our route passes through Holybred Wood, a beautiful stretch of mature woodland with hornbeams, holly and wild service trees. There are bluebells in the spring and woodpeckers are supposedly common, although we did not see or hear one. The Little Baddow Millennium Walk, which our route coincides with very briefly, is a circuit of around seven miles passing through some of the other woods.

After the optional loop, the walk takes you past Ulting church which, in the Middle Ages, was a busy pilgrimage destination associated with a statue of the Virgin Mary. Recently, it has been the focus of a minor local conflict because the churchyard was a popular spot to picnic and swim, but the vicar objected to this. We could see a tempting lawn, but with so much accessible river close by there is clearly no need to swim just there.

The last part of the walk heads through fields and small woods, past some fishing ponds to reach Hatfield Peverel near the site of a Benedictine priory, said to have been founded by Ingelrica, the Saxon wife of Ranulph Peverel, to atone for her sins – especially that of being mistress to William the Conqueror. Little remains of the priory except the name, attached to an 18th century house nearby, and part of the parish church of St Andrews. The Peverel that the town is named after is probably Ranulph's son, William, who may have fought in the Battle of Hastings and to whom William the Conqueror granted land. However, the long history suggested by the name has left few traces in the present.

DIRECTIONS

❶ HATFIELD PEVEREL

From the station keep straight ahead to cross a bridge over the A12 and turn right onto the B1137. Turn left into Church Road after the Swan pub. Follow the road past the cricket ground then look for a signed footpath through a kissing gate on the right immediately after the Scout and Guide hut. Follow the path with allotments on the right, then fields on both sides.

1 mile

❷ OVER A STREAM

Briefly join a minor road to pass a thatched house on the left, continuing on the footpath ahead. After about 150 metres the path crosses a stream. Take the straight path up the field along the left side of the hedge. Continue until you reach a lane. Turn right, pass one house and look for the footpath on the left.

1.5 miles

❸ TO PAPER MILL BRIDGE

After crossing a bridge over a ditch, ignore a cart track on the left and continue diagonally across two fields towards a house (Botters Farm) and thatched barn. Take the path to the right of the barn. After a stile and a little bridge take the left-hand path downhill. At the bottom, bear right to pass a breezeblock barn on your left and take the path half-left diagonally across a field. On the far side continue right on the path with a hedgerow on the left. Continue ahead on a tarmac track. At the road, turn left to cross the Chelmer Navigation by Paper Mill Bridge.

2.5 miles

❹ ROUTE OPTIONS

(a) The shortcut

Turn left downstream after the bridge on a river path. After half a mile near a bend in the river a path from the right is where the main route joins. Continue the directions from 6, and deduct three miles from subsequent distances.

(b) The main route

Turn right on the footpath along the far side of the river, passing Paper Mill Lock, the Stables café and narrowboat moorings. Follow the river path upstream, noticing a church, St Mary the Virgin, across the fields. When you can see the road bridge ahead, turn left on a marked footpath just before a footbridge where a stream joins the main river. Follow the path across the fields towards the church you saw earlier. Cross the footpath below the graveyard and pass to the right of the church.

4 miles

❺ AROUND LITTLE BADDOW

On reaching the road turn left. Continue until you pass the United Reformed Church, then turn left on the footpath in front of the house on the opposite side of the road; the path may be slightly overgrown. After crossing a bridge over a ditch, keep left of the telegraph pole to pick up a cart track that leads across the field, with Holybreds Farm some distance away to the right. At a T-junction with another path turn left and soon right over a small bridge with a handrail, briefly joining the signed Little Baddow

Millennium Walk. Enter Holybred Wood and leave the Millennium Walk at the signed footpath to the right. Walk up through the wood to the road and turn left. Continue past some newish houses to North Hill where you turn left and immediately right into Tofts Chase. After some way, look for a footpath sign by an oak tree on the left, opposite a small house. The path crosses fields to the Chelmer. At the bottom of the last field, turn right along a faint path that skirts a thicket to join the river. This is where the shortcut rejoins the main route. Just downstream there is a bench and a good entry point to the river – an ideal spot for a picnic and swim.

6 miles

❻ BESIDE THE CHELMER

Walk on downstream passing a high arched footbridge, a lock and Ulting church on the far bank. This is an idyllic place to swim. Find a gap in the vegetation on the bank and expect a bit of a scramble to get out.

7.5 miles

❼ CROSSING THE CHELMER

Cross the bridge over a side channel by a weir. On reaching the road at Hoe Mill (note the information board about the history of the area), turn left to cross the Chelmer and right onto a path along the north bank. Soon there is a seat and then, at a slight bend in the river, another good swimming place.

8.5 miles

❽ PAST FISHING PONDS

Look for a signed footpath on the left, which skirts a gravel pit reserved for fishing. Don't be tempted by the broad ride: the path veers right to cross a stream and shortly meets a road. Cross and continue up the left-hand side of a field. Cross a stream to enter the next field taking the path to the right. Pass the corner of a reservoir on the left, resist the appealing path along the side of the lake and instead follow the path that goes right, later with a hedge on your left. Continue along the right-hand side of the final field. On reaching the road turn left to reach a slightly more main road.

9.5 miles

❾ TOWARDS HATFIELD PEVEREL

Turn right, pass a house (Couchman's) and look on the left for an overgrown footpath sign. Follow the path parallel to the road with a metal fence on the left. At the far corner of the fence turn left, keeping it on your left and later pass another flooded gravel pit on your left. Follow the path, which veers right to become a grassy ride between a hornbeam hedge and a wood of oak and alder, then leaves the grassy ride to the left and continues between a fence and a hedge to a road.

10 miles

❿ INTO HATFIELD PEVEREL

Turn left, then right into Sportsmans Lane. Take the signed footpath to the right between hedges. The path continues with a

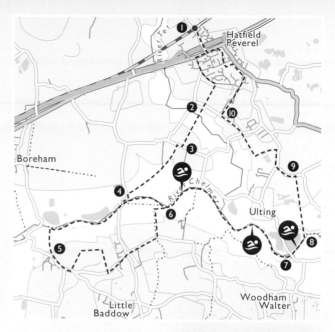

field on the right, passes the grounds of a big house, the Priory, to the left and then the cemetery of St Andrew's church. After passing allotments turn left at the path T-junction to reach the road. Turn right here. Walk past the school and just beyond the entrance to the junior school turn left on the path between neatly clipped high hedges. Follow the tarmac path along the length of the recreation ground and, after bending around the end of the ground, leave at the far corner. Continue along the path for about 50 metres until there is a path on the right (opposite a lamp post). Follow the path across several residential roads to the main street

of Hatfield Peverel (B1137), almost opposite Station Road. Retrace your steps to the station.

11 miles

Margaret Dickinson, Liz Valentine, Ros Bayley.

Walk 9

MANNINGTREE CIRCULAR, ESSEX AND SUFFOLK

A beautiful walk through Constable country with several opportunities to enjoy good river swimming in the famous Stour.

INFORMATION

DISTANCE: 7.25 miles.
TIME: 3.5 to 4 hours.
MAPS: OS Landranger 168 (Colchester); OS Explorer 184 (Colchester) and 196 (Sudbury, Hadleigh & Dedham Vale).
START AND END POINT: Manningtree Railway Station.
PUBLIC TRANSPORT: By train from Liverpool Street or Stratford.
SWIMMING: In the River Stour.
PLACES OF INTEREST: St Mary's church, Lawford; Dedham village; Flatford Mill and Willy Lott's House; Flatford wildlife sanctuary.
REFRESHMENTS: There is a buffet/bar on Manningtree Station; Dedham is full of pubs and restaurants; a good National Trust café at Flatford Mill (CO7 6UL, tel 01206 298260).
ROWING BOAT HIRE: Flatford and Dedham, tel 01206 323153.

This walk is a delightful way to experience Constable country. The painter grew up in the nearby village of East Bergholt, the son of a prosperous miller who owned the water mills at Dedham and Flatford. Flatford Mill is now a busy tourist destination but the visitors do not wander far so you can walk nearly all the way passing few people, yet immersed in landscapes that still look remarkably like Constable's.

We walked there in June on an unsettled day of those bubbling cloudscapes the painter is famous for, when the meadows were golden with buttercups, glorious to see. We did the walk again on a perfect August day with sunshine, blue sky and white fluffy clouds. Some cornfields had been harvested. Families were picnicking and swimming and many people were rowing boats on the river. Swallows followed us all the way, dipping over the fields, while others gathered on the wires in readiness for their long journey. House martins were nesting under the bridge at Flatford and also at Manningtree station. We saw rooks and green woodpeckers in the fields, Egyptian geese, mallards and a little grebe in the Stour, a flock of goldfinches including fluffy juveniles feasting on thistles, and greenfinches and a couple of whitethroats. We heard but could not see a blackcap. There were also many butterflies (Red Admiral, Peacock, Small Tortoiseshell, Speckled Wood, Meadow Brown, Gatekeeper and Common Blue) as well as a few dragonflies.

There are plenty of places to swim in the Stour between Dedham and Flatford, but a particularly good spot is opposite Dedham Mill ❹ where the river opens into a pond and there is a small gravelly beach. The water is shallow at the edge and you have to paddle out some way before you can swim, but then a few strokes will take you out of your depth. Further down towards Flatford you need to be careful because the river is not wide and may be busy with small boats.

There is a lot to see on the way. St Mary's church in Lawford ❶, probably built as the estate church of Lawford Hall, dates from the 14th century. The tower is composed of a delightful mixture of brick and different kinds of stone including pudding-stone, and the light, spacious interior is well worth a visit. Pevsner describes the early 14th century chancel as 'one of the most splendid monuments of its date in the county'.

Dedham ❸ is an attractive village with old pubs and houses and its parish church, also dedicated to St Mary, is one of the great churches of the area – a grand, mainly 15th century building, testimony to the prosperous weaving industry. The tower was painted several times by Constable and the church contains one of Constable's very few religious paintings, the Ascension.

Dedham Mill, built in 1809, was owned by Golding Constable, the painter's father, and used for grinding grain and making cloth. An unfinished painting by Constable, sometimes on show at Tate Britain, depicts a rustic building considerably smaller than the structure there today and surrounded by more open ground.

The hamlet of Flatford ❺, by contrast, preserves several buildings more or less as Constable painted them. The effect is slightly disturbing, as if the last 200 years, which transformed economic and social life, had never happened. No doubt the effect is partly achieved by restoration undertaken by the National Trust, which acquired the estate in 1943. Bridge Cottage, next to the National Trust café, now houses a small Constable exhibition. Beyond the café is the dry dock depicted in Constable's 'Boat Building on the Stour' – or at least a dry dock that looks similar. The Mill and Willy Lott's House are a little further downstream and the latter, particularly, looks very like the painting of it.

DIRECTIONS

❶ MANNINGTREE

Turn right out of the station and go down the slope to a footpath signed to Flatford and Dedham. At the tarmac track, turn right and almost at once take a signed footpath left leading uphill with fields to the left and trees to the right. At the top of the hill the path bears right and continues to St Mary's church. From here all the way to Dedham the route follows the Essex Way (EW).

❷ ON THE ESSEX WAY

Go through the churchyard and out the other side to a lane where there are two FP signs. Take the left hand path, which follows the field edge (keeping the fence on your left) out to a road junction. Turn right up Dedham Road until you come to two FP signs on the left. Follow the left-hand one, which bears slightly right, and aim across the field to the left of a pylon. (If there is a standing crop, you may have to go round the field edge.) Continue past a cross path to a track onto which you turn left, bearing to the right and then straight on following the EW (avoiding a left turn). Continue on

this green lane to a house on the right (Humberlands). Immediately afterwards, take a signed footpath to the right which leads into a small wood and soon crosses a small stream and then the railway track. Take care: this is the main Norwich line, with fast trains on it.

1.5 miles

❸ TO DEDHAM

Continue straight on across a large meadow, with horses often in it, through several kissing gates to cross a road. Continue on the path, from where you get your first view of Dedham church and glimpses of the beautiful Stour valley, to another road, where you turn right and walk down through trees to take a path on the left at the bottom just before a bend in the road. Follow it to a fairly busy road. Turn right and at a safe point cross over to take a path on the left. After passing through four fields, turn right on a surfaced lane ignoring a path straight on. Go down the lane a short distance, passing some cottages and take a left turning (FP and EW signs) that almost at once becomes a path. Continue by Park Farm, keeping left, avoiding a couple of paths to the right. Soon cross a small stream bed and shortly afterwards take a path off to the right, heading towards Dedham church. At the cricket ground a path turns left but stay on the EW, which turns right then left, emerging onto a road just east of Dedham church.

3.5 miles

❹ A SWIM IN THE STOUR

Take the road opposite the church (B1029, Mill Lane) and follow it to cross the River Stour. For a short diversion to a good swimming place and picnic spot, take the path to the left along the river to arrive opposite Dedham Mill.

❺ TO FLATFORD

Afterwards, retrace your steps to the road and cross over to take the path opposite, which follows the Stour downstream towards Flatford Mill. From here to Manningtree station, the route follows the St Edmund Way. After about half a mile, the path crosses the river by a footbridge and continues along the right bank to another bridge. Cross and turn right on a narrow road to reach the National Trust Centre, Bridge Cottage, Willy Lott's House and Flatford Mill itself.

6 miles

❻ RETURN TO MANNINGTREE

After exploring the mill area, retrace your steps to Bridge Cottage and cross back over the little bridge, turn left and continue downstream on the river's right bank. After passing Willy Lott's House on the far side of the river ignore a path to the left (a dead end) and continue following the river, but at a slight distance. From here on, access to the river for swimming becomes difficult. The path crosses a small tributary stream and veers to the left, with another path going off to the right. Take the left-hand path (signed Manningtree) and a little further on cross another small tributary where the path curves slightly left, still following the river. You will soon see a path off to the right, which should be signposted to Manningtree station, but on our second visit all three fingerposts had been broken off. This soon becomes a track, which zigzags its way back to Manningtree station.

7.25 miles

Margaret Dickinson, Liz Valentine.

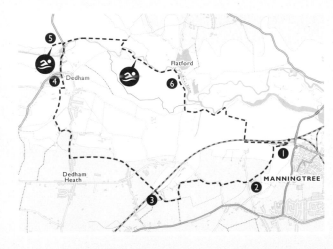

Walk 10

HEVER TO LEIGH, KENT

An easy walk through beautiful countryside, passing Kentish Wealden houses and several places of historical interest along the way, with a swim in the River Medway.

INFORMATION

DISTANCE: 7.5 miles.
TIME: 3 hours.
MAP: OS Landranger 188 (Maidstone & Royal Tunbridge Wells); OS Explorer 147 (Sevenoaks & Tonbridge).
START POINT: Hever Station.
END POINT: Leigh Station.
PUBLIC TRANSPORT: Train from London Bridge to Hever; return from Leigh to London Victoria (or Charing Cross by changing at Tonbridge).
REFRESHMENTS: King Henry VIII pub, Hever (TN8 7NG, tel 01732 862457); Fir Tree House Tea Rooms, Penshurst (TN11 8DB tel 01892 870382); Porcupine Café, Penshurst Place (TN11 8DG tel 01892 870307); Fleur de Lys pub, Leigh.
SWIMMING: In the River Medway.
PLACES OF INTEREST: Hever Castle; St Mary's church, Hever; Penshurst Place; St John the Baptist church, Penshurst; St Mary's church, Leigh (TN11 8RL tel 01732 832235).

The pleasure of this walk begins the moment you alight from the train at the tiny station in Hever, the path rising from the embankment directly into the wooded countryside. In May the walk is stunning, the path weaving through clouds of cow parsley and an abundance of wild flowers. We saw honeysuckle, herb robert, wild geraniums, buttercups, vetch, red campion, foxgloves, pinky white hawthorn blossom and carpets of bluebells. It's a wonderful walk for foraging, with succulent nettles, dandelions and the heady smell of wild garlic. In September there were plenty of blackberries, autumnal red berries, a Comma butterfly, and – the greatest excitement – a pair of kingfishers flashing past, caught in the sunlight, near the swimming place.

The Medway here is quite narrow and cleaner than the busy waterway that runs through Maidstone – and completely unlike the great tidal river it has become by the time it passes Rochester, Chatham and Gillingham on its way to the Thames. Yet even in these upper reaches the Medway was once important for communications and for powering mills. The channel, which was made navigable up to Tonbridge in the 18th century, was improved up to Leigh in the 19th century, but in recent years the banks have become very overgrown in places.

On the way to the swim the route passes some impressive churches and great houses. Hever Castle, a moated and crenellated sandstone structure dating back to the 13th century, was the home of the Boleyn, Waldegrave and Astor families at various periods. The name Hever is derived from the Saxon 'Heanyfre' meaning 'high edge'. The castle and Italianate gardens are open

house in all England', it is a 14th century manor house and gardens. It once belonged to Henry VIII (it was given to Anne of Cleves as part of her divorce settlement) and was then home to the Sidney family from 1552 for 460 years (Sir Philip Sidney was born here). The state rooms are open from the end of March to the beginning of November; the garden is open all year.

from April to October but it would be ambitious to combine a full visit with the walk. We would, however, recommend slipping into St Mary's church in Hever, a splendid building dating from the 13th century containing several important brasses, in particular those of Margaret Cheyne (died 1419) and Sir Thomas Bullen (died 1538), father of Anne Boleyn.

Just over halfway the route passes Penshurst Place ❺. Described as 'the grandest and most perfectly preserved example of a fortified manor

Two more churches compete for attention. The church of St John the Baptist in Penshurst is a yellow sandstone building boasting a font unusually painted in bright colours, the Sidney chapel with its painted vaulted ceiling, and many interesting monuments. Thomas Becket was a priest there. A booklet on the history of the village and church are on sale inside.

St Mary's church, Leigh (pronounced 'lie') dates from the 13th century. It underwent some reconstruction in the 1860s, and notable features include a 14th century stained glass, a 16th century brass, an hour-glass stand and Flemish wood carving on the lectern.

DIRECTIONS

This route follows the Eden Valley Walk (EVW), which is marked on the OS map and well signposted.

❶ HEVER VILLAGE

Upon leaving the station, cross the bridge over the railway and turn left on the path (EVW) by the railway. Pass Bayleaf Hall. On reaching the road, turn left back over the railway. At the

T-junction continue straight on (FP signed EVW), passing a lake on your right and a Wealden house on your left. At the road, turn right and then take the first left (signposted Hever Castle), opposite the bus shelter. At the top of the hill you will find the Henry VIII pub and Hever church.

I mile

❷ HEVER TO HOATH

Pass through the churchyard and continue on this path, which later becomes a track with Park Wood on your left, until you reach Bothy Cottages on your right. Here the path forks right at the gate of one of the cottages. On reaching the road, carry on straight across on the path, crossing a stream and continuing uphill through a wooded area. Cross the bridleway and continue through the woods, through a steep gulley and when the path opens out into a large meadow area, watch for the signpost at the centre of the meadow and bear right to the hamlet of Hill Hoath.

2.5 miles

❸ SLIPS WOOD

Turn right at the road junction, taking a path immediately on your left. Bear left at Hill Hoath House and soon right at a path junction. Continue on through a wood (The Slips), crossing a stream. On reaching the B road, turn right then left to stay on the EVW. Walk diagonally across the field and turn left into a minor road (bridleway). Continue straight on to Wat Stock. There is an ideal place for lunch here with a seat round a tree and a lovely view over the Eden valley.

3.5 miles

❹ TO PENSHURST PLACE

Continue straight on, enjoying the lovely views to your left, finally joining a tarmac road across open country to cross the River Eden. At the main road turn left, then take the first FP sharp right to pass Penshurst Place on your left and reach Penshurst church.

4.75 miles

❺ PAST PENSHURST PLACE

Pass through the timbered medieval passage (with the inscription 'My flesh also shall rest in hope') and turn left onto the road to enter the grounds of Penshurst Place. At the end of the boundary wall you can turn off to the left to the shop and tea room for a welcome cuppa. Rejoin the path and, after passing a small lake on your left, look out for a squeezer stile on your left. Bearing right, follow this path uphill (look back for a view of

Penshurst Place) where you continue straight on, ignoring a path on the left. At a red brick house on the right (marked Killick's Bank on the Explorer map) fork right on the FP through another squeezer stile.

6 miles

❻ A SWIM IN THE MEDWAY

This takes you down to cross a bridge and another field to the River Medway. Turn left here and look for a place to swim as you approach Ensfield Bridge. There are two spots, close together and near the bridge, opposite the row of poplar trees. You can swim either from a ledge close to the water, or enter the river where the ground dips down to water level. We were told by locals to take care under the bridge itself because there are objects in the river.

6.5 miles

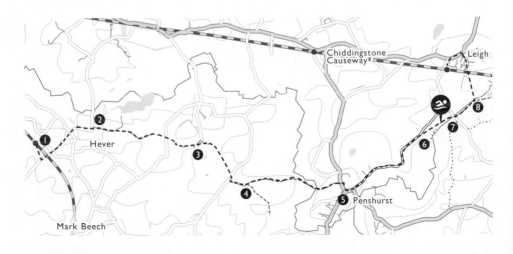

❼ BESIDE THE MEDWAY

If you're short of time, the direct route to Leigh station is to turn left along this B road. Otherwise, cross the road and follow the EVW parallel to the river on its right bank, to pass through a beautiful wooded area. Continue on a track through fields, until you reach a path crossing at the beginning of Straight Mile.

7 miles

❽ INTO LEIGH

Leaving the EVW, turn left here on a FP that bears left to cross the river on a Bailey bridge.

Keep straight ahead through two fields, going under the railway and up to join a residential road. Continue along this road to reach the green at the far end. Turn left and look out for Crandalls Road on your left. Take this, continuing through a housing area, turning left into Well Close, which emerges onto the main road just before Leigh station. Alternatively, visit Leigh church, visible beyond the green on an eminence overlooking the village. Then turn right (west) out of the church, continue down the High Street to the

Fleurs de Lis pub, where you turn left for the station.

7.5 miles

Liz Valentine, Sarah Saunders.

Walk 11

CHILWORTH TO GUILDFORD, SURREY

This fairly easy walk crosses heathland dotted with pretty Surrey villages before dropping down to follow the Wey Navigation, where there are many swimming places.

T he route starts by crossing a strange mixture of wild and rather forbidding heathland of scrub and gorse, but soon gives way to gentle pastures, small woods and cosy commuter villages. UK heathland is actually very rare and precious, and this heath provides a unique habitat for ground-nesting birds and rare invertebrates among the characteristic plants like bell heather and ling that thrive on these poor, sandy soils. Once thinly populated and devoid of large villages or great houses, the weaving of coarse woollen cloth brought some prosperity to the area along the Wey in the late Middle Ages, but this cottage industry fell victim to competition from London Guilds in the 17th century, leaving high unemployment.

In the 19th century, however, when middle class Londoners began to establish weekend retreats or commuter homes along the new railway lines, the very poverty of the area was an attraction. Low land prices, romantic, uninhabited landscapes and hamlets that looked untouched by industrialisation made it a favoured destination, particularly to those inspired by the Arts and Crafts movement with its nostalgia for a preindustrial England of vernacular architecture and handmade products. The prosperous incomers renovated the crumbling remains of weaving sheds, knocked cottages together, commissioned new houses around existing villages, or arranged them in new 'ancient' villages. Where the work was heavily influenced by Arts and Crafts sensibilities, these 19th and early 20th century buildings are often hard to distinguish from the much older models. Blackheath village ❷, where much of the work was done by the architect Charles Harrison Townsend, is a good example.

INFORMATION

DISTANCE: 8 miles.
TIME: 4 hours.
MAP: OS Landranger 186 (Aldershot & Guildford) or OS Explorer 145 (Guildford & Farnham)
START POINT: Chilworth Station.
END POINT: Guildford Station.
PUBLIC TRANSPORT: Trains from Waterloo; change at Guildford for Chilworth. Several trains an hour to Guildford, but infrequent service to Chilworth.
SWIMMING: Several places in the Wey Navigation.
PLACES OF INTEREST: Blackheath, Arts and Crafts houses in Blackheath; Wonersh church; Wey Navigation; Dapdune Wharf, Guildford.
REFRESHMENTS: Village stores and Grantley Arms (GU5 0PE tel 01483 893351) in Wonersh; Hectors on the Wey café, Farncombe Boat House (GU7 1NH, tel 01483 418769); The Manor Inn Beefeater GU7 3BX tel 01483 427134); The Britannia (GU2 4BE, tel 01483 572160) and The White House pubs (GU2 4AJ, tel 01483 302006), Guildford.
BOAT HIRE: Rowing boats and canoes (also narrowboats) from Farncombe Boat House, Catteshall (GU7 1NH, tel 01483 421306).

Chilworth has a less genteel history, owing its growth to a gunpowder works established in 1625 by the East India Company. The works closed in 1920 but some buildings remain. Wonersh boasts some original early English buildings (of Bargate stone, timber-framed and tile-hung) and good Arts and Crafts architecture, as well as a lot of indifferent later housing. St John the Baptist's church ❸ is worth visiting for the beautiful meadow in front and its gateway with an interesting relief, the inspiration and design for which originated with Beatrice E Lock and was developed and carried out by John Hurren, both local residents. The church, which was locked when we visited, was restored in the 18th century and again in 1902, but contains older fragments (part of the north wall is pre-Conquest and the base of the tower is 12th century).

When we did the walk in late April, village gardens were bursting with blossom, banks were covered with the white stars of stitchwort and some of the woods, particularly the one between Bramley and Cateshall ❹-❺, were filled with bluebells and wild garlic. In June, there were foxgloves, buttercups, wild roses and the poisonous hemlock water dropwort. We saw swallows and house martins and heard a garden warbler and a reed bunting. Pairs of Banded Demoiselle damselflies courted along the Wey Navigation and a Small Tortoiseshell butterfly fluttered by in the warm sunshine.

Once the route joins the Wey Navigation ❺ it follows the towpath right into Guildford and almost to the station. The Wey was only the second river in England to be turned from wholly unnavigable to wholly navigable. The section from Weybridge to Guildford was opened in 1653 but the extension to Godalming was only completed in 1764. It is now used for leisure by canal barges and canoeists.

Swimming is quite well established as a local pastime and two spots in particular seem popular.

The first occurs very soon after reaching the Wey, just beyond the Manor Inn ❺, and is a tiny patch of sandy beach where someone has placed poles, presumably to warn non-swimmers not to go on into deep water. We swam here and it was a pleasant surprise. The weather had turned cold and the water looked grey and uninviting, but as soon as we plunged past the marker poles it became clear why – on warmer days – it is so popular. The water was deep and much cleaner than it appeared from the bank and even in the dull light was full of reflections of trees and sky. There is only a slight current, but one hazard to look out for is the narrowboats, especially those drawn by horses that have limited scope to manoeuvre.

Just after this beach there is a pretty stretch with better cover for changing but less easy access. The next main swimming place is close to Guildford and has a more extensive sandy beach and also a steep sandy bank, which looks as if children love to race down and splash into the water. There are other places too, but less suitable for children. St Catherine's Lock ❻ has lovely deep water but lacks access spots, although a little downstream there is a possible entry place.

DIRECTIONS

❶ CHILWORTH AND BLACKHEATH

Turn right out of station along a main road signed to Dorking. Take the first signed footpath (Downs Link) on the right after some houses and follow it uphill. For a time the footpath and a bridleway run parallel. At a junction of paths by Lingwood House, take a right-hand fork on a sandy track over Blackheath, which soon passes a war memorial on the left. On reaching a minor road turn left to the tiny village of Blackheath and continue over a crossroad. (Note the amusing signpost pointing to This way, That way and Somewhere else.)

1 mile

❷ TO WONERSH

As you leave the village ignore some small unsigned paths to the right but take a signed bridleway on the right (the right-hand fork of two paths). This later joins the Fox Way, is signed by blue-marked posts and descends a steep gully, with a wire fence on your left. You pass Lynes Farm (on the right) at the bottom of the valley. Continue uphill on an enclosed path to reach a cemetery on your left. Cross the track here and continue uphill (SW), bearing left when you meet a fence and a path coming in from the right. Pass Barnett Hill Conference Centre on your right and continue downhill

towards Wonersh. At a minor road, turn left and then at the main road turn right. At the next junction bear left on a road signposted to Bramley.

2.5 miles

❸ TO BRAMLEY

A short way down the road go through a red brick crenellated gateway to the walled church green and the church of St John the Baptist. Note the stone frieze carved by local resident John Hurren in 1953. Return to the road and continue towards Bramley, passing the old Bramley & Wonersh station, to reach a main road.

3 miles

❹ INTO THE WEY VALLEY

At the main road turn right and then turn left along a lane indicated by a bridleway sign. The lane soon turns into a path that continues ahead between a gate marked private and a driveway. Follow the path uphill and on as it levels out and continues with a golf course on the right. Cross a little road and continue on the bridleway the other side, up a hill with a training track for racehorses on the right and on the left a wood, which in season is full of bluebells. The path is fenced in until shortly after the top of the hill when it soon starts to drop into the Wey valley. At the bottom of the hill, it is crossed by a track. Turn right here downhill, bearing left onto a bridleway at the next junction shortly afterwards, by the

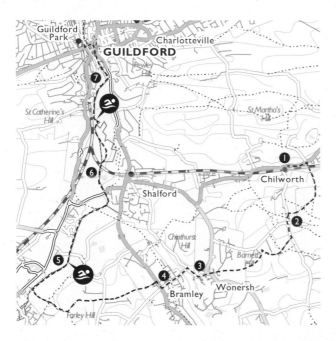

driveway to Bunkers Hill Farm. On reaching the river Wey, cross over Trowers Bridge and turn right. After a short distance pass the Manor Inn on the left. After that the river and the path leave houses behind and there are some good places to swim. One is a little sandy beach with a line of poles marking the start of deep water.
5 miles

❺ THE WEY TOWPATH

From here the route is straightforward. Shortly after the swimming place the Navigation is crossed by a bridge carrying a minor road. After passing Unstead Lock you cross a disused railway line. You pass Stonebridge by a junction of waterways and next cross the A248 at Broadford Bridge.
6.5 miles

❻ APPROACH TO GUILDFORD

The next bridge carries the railway from Guildford to Chilworth and beyond. Soon after this is St Catherine's Lock where there are possible but slightly difficult swimming places. There is an easier and popular sandy spot further on where the left bank becomes steep and wooded, just before a footbridge that carries the North Downs Way over the Navigation. Shortly after this the first houses of Guildford appear on the left.
7 miles

❼ GUILDFORD

The path continues, reaching a pleasant picnicking meadow between two waterways, at Millmead Lock. It then crosses two bridges, bringing you into the centre of Guildford. Go on past the church. Just before a bridge the station is signed to the left, but it is preferable to ignore this sign and continue along the Navigation to take the next left turning up some steps, which brings you out close to the station.
8 miles

Margaret Dickinson, Liz Valentine.

Walk 12

WINCHFIELD TO HOOK, HAMPSHIRE

This pretty walk offers swims in a trout stream and a spring-fed canal, and passes lakes, nature reserves, churches, a mill and a ruined castle.

*W*e first did this walk on a sunny April day when the scenery seemed to be all white blossom, green buds and shimmering water, but in any season water is a strong theme as it is never far away. A second theme is history and, unsurprisingly, the two are linked.

The route includes two sections of the Three Castles Path, a long distance trail between Windsor and Winchester inspired by the journeys King John made from his castle in Odiham. These sections follow the Basingstoke Canal, a narrow, pretty waterway, mostly tree lined and rather meandering for a canal. Completed in 1794, it was built to promote agricultural development and linked Basingstoke to the Wey Navigation in West Byfleet, which in turn links to the Thames. Barges carried flour, timber and chalk out and brought in coal and fertiliser, but as a commercial venture it was a failure and the company went bankrupt in 1866.

Parts remained navigable until the mid 20th century when it fell into complete disrepair and might have disappeared, had it not been for the hard work of the Surrey and Hampshire Canal Society. Formed in 1966, the society campaigned successfully for the two county councils to buy it and contribute towards its restoration, which was completed in 1991. Details can be found on the Basingstoke Canal Society's website.

Our walk joins the canal twice, first along a stretch crossed by attractive bridges with nameplates dated 1792 ❷, and the second time by the Greywell Tunnel ❽, which collapsed in 1932 and now marks the end of the canal. There is no towpath through the tunnel, so barges used to push their barges through by lying on their backs and pressing their feet against the wall.

INFORMATION

DISTANCE: 11 miles (9.5 miles with shortcut).
TIME: 6 hours.
MAP: OS Landranger (186 Aldershot & Guildford); OS Explorer 144 (Basingstoke, Alton & Whitchurch).
START POINT: Winchfield Station.
END POINT: Hook Station.
PUBLIC TRANSPORT: Train from Waterloo.
SWIMMING: River Whitewater, a trout stream, and in Basingstoke Canal.
PLACES OF INTEREST: The Basingstoke Canal; St Mary the Virgin, Winchfield; All Saints church, Odiham; St Mary's church, Greywell; Odiham Castle; Greywell Mill; Greywell Moors wetland reserve; Bartley Heath nature reserve.
REFRESHMENTS: The Bell (RG29 1LY, tel 01256 702282) and The Crown, a pub with a well-reviewed Bangladeshi restaurant (RG29 1PH, tel 01256 702489), both Odiham; The Fox and Goose, Greywell (RG29 1BY, tel 01256 702062); The Mill House pub, Warnborough (RG29 1ET, tel 01256 702953).

The blocked tunnel is now significant as a haunt of five species of bats.

One of the swimming places is in the canal near the tunnel. The canal is fed from chalk springs which is why the water quality, in this part at least, is unusually good. We swam in a wide, deep section almost opposite Odiham Castle ❽. The water was pleasantly clear but very cold. Another place to swim, a little earlier in the walk, is in the River Whitewater just downstream from Greywell Mill ❼. The water is sparkling clear and also very cold, but fast-flowing and shallow in places. The banks can be a little muddy and you need to be aware that it is a trout stream where you may meet anglers.

After the first section of canal the walk passes two lovely lakes, but neither is that suitable for swimming. Tundry Pond, in the grounds of Dog-mersfield Park Hotel, has two parts. The smaller is reserved for fishing, lined with 'No swimming' signs, and feels under observation, but there are benches there making it a pleasant picnic spot. The larger pond is free of 'No swimming' signs, as far as we could see, and is warmer than the later swimming places but rather shallow, little more than three feet deep. One of our walkers found the whole area with its signs and fences

a little sinister. According to local legend, its present charm does hide a dark history because a village was supposedly cleared to make way for the ponds. Further on, Dogmersfield Lake is private and directly overlooked by Aragon Hall.

Throughout the walk nature and culture compete for interest. The route passes three fine medieval churches. St Mary the Virgin in Winchfield has a remarkable Norman chancel and Norman doorway. All Saints at Odiham has a Saxon foundation, but the present building dates mainly from the 13th, 15th, 16th and 17th centuries, with the lovely brick tower rebuilt in the 17th century. St Mary's in Greywell dates from the 12th century, is screened by great yew trees in a secluded churchyard and inside has a beautiful early 16th century wooden rood screen. Odiham Castle, built by King John on a bend in the River Whitewater, is now a romantic ruin.

The latter part of the walk goes through two nature reserves: Greywell Moors ❼ is an area of fen and wet woodland along the Whitewater where several kinds of orchids grow in early summer. Bartley Heath ❿ and Hook Common are areas of common land, with a long history of livestock grazing, where cattle and ponies are now used to help manage the heathland for wildlife.

DIRECTIONS

❶ WINCHFIELD
Turn left out of the station on a suburban road which winds through redbrick houses and past a lily pond, then leads to a pedestrian-only way through to a busier minor road. Turn right and

then at the next junction right again. Continue to the church of St Mary the Virgin on the left. Go through the churchyard to find a signed path on the far side through a kissing gate. Go through a wood, Hellet's Copse, which has bluebells

in spring and is full of songbirds in early summer, then cross a field to reach the canal. Do not cross the bridge but go left onto the towpath and turn right under Stacey's Bridge.
1.5 miles

② THE BASINGSTOKE CANAL

Continue under Baseley's Bridge and leave the canal at the next bridge, Sprat's Hatch Bridge.
2 miles

③ TUNDRY POND

Cross the bridge and take a waymarked footpath veering slightly left onto a farm track. Pass Sprat's Hatch Farm. Go through a kissing gate beside big gates for Dogmersfield Park Estate and walk along a track that later becomes a hard track between numerous 'Beware of the bull' signs (we did not notice these on our first visit). Divert to the left over a meadow to visit Tundry Pond.
2.5 miles

④ DOGMERSFIELD ESTATE

From the pond, walk back along the hard track and take a signed and fenced path obliquely to the right between the track and a driveway. At a large gate follow a sign to the left of it. Continue on the path through a wood by Dogmersfield Lake, watched over by Aragon Hall. Walk down the driveway to a very busy road (A287) and turn left for a few yards.
4 miles

⑤ TO ODIHAM

Cross the road and take a rather poorly marked path on the right in a wooded area just to the left of a driveway. Fairly soon, just after a path off to the right before a fenced field on the right, take a signed path to the right through a little gate. Cross a field to a gate the other side. Cross a drive and continue on a signed path that does not go through a gate ahead but turns slightly right between a fence and hedge. Ignore a sign to the left very soon, but a little later take a signed path over a stile

on the left. Continue to cross a bridge over a small stream and follow the path over swamp-prone ground, then up a slight incline to the first houses of Odiham. The path runs between ends of the back gardens of these houses, and a large field full of poppies in summer. When the path ends at a main road, turn right and almost at once take a lane left, signed to Odiham cottage hospital. Walk past the hospital and on to find All Saints church on the right. Go through the churchyard to a square where you can see The Bell.
5.5 miles

⑥ ODIHAM TO THE WHITEWATER

Before the square, just after the church, turn left along a hard surfaced path to a road where, on the right, is The Crown. Cross the road and go straight on along a path between gardens. At the end turn right into a minor road and then left onto a busier road. Pass Robert May's School on the right. Cross the road and take a path right with the school building on the right. As you near the end of the buildings take a path left over a stile and head across the field, veering a little right of straight on, looking out for stiles into a lane on the far side. There are two stiles. Take the one more to the right to cross the lane and continue on the footpath that cuts across to a road at right angles to the lane, runs beside this and then turns right to cross it. If this bit of path is very overgrown, just turn right down the lane after crossing the stile, then left at the road towards Upton Grey. Very soon there is a right turning, Deptford Lane, to Greywell. Pass this and just afterwards you will pick up the footpath on the right. This takes you over another field, through

which the footpath is very clear, and towards a wooded valley. On other side of the field, you will find yourself on Greywell Moors.
7 miles

⑦ ROUTE OPTIONS

The shortcut (saves just under 1.5 miles). Go through a metal gate and straight on through a small nature reserve to cross a bridge over the clear, bright waters of the Whitewater – look out for trout here. Head up and diagonally towards the top of the path that leads down to the church then rejoins the longer route.
The main route. Go through the metal gate and turn off left through another gate. Walk along the edge of a nature reserve of wooded wetlands. After about three quarters of a mile take a path that turns off to the right so sharply as to almost double back. It is a little hard to spot and seems an odd direction, but it is right if it leads to a trout pool on the left then to a mill house ahead, Greywell Mill. Just after the mill turn left then immediately right onto a path by the Whitewater. We swam a little way along here.
8 miles

⑧ GREYWELL VILLAGE AND ODIHAM CASTLE

Follow the stream then turn away left through the churchyard of St Mary's, Greywell to meet the shortcut. Go past the church, leave the churchyard and turn left to a nearby road. Turn right on the road to walk though the attractive village of Greywell past the Fox and Goose pub. Go straight on at a T-junction and just afterward the canal appears on the right. Turn right to join the towpath and you will see Greywell

Tunnel behind you. Continue along the canal to the ruins of Odiham Castle and the swimming place.
9 miles

9 NORTH WARNBOROUGH

Shortly after the castle turn left through a metal kissing gate, through a field to a road. Turn left and, where the road fords the Whitewater, cross on a footbridge. Go past a green, cross a second branch of the river and veer right along a lane beside a small stream into North Warnborough. At the next junction bear right, follow the road round to the B3349. (You can divert right here to visit the Mill House pub, which has an attractive garden and, inside, the old mill wheel is preserved). Otherwise, cross and continue on a concrete path. Where the concrete runs out bear left,

leaving to the right another path over a bridge. Cross the field to a gate where you cross a waterway and go under the main A287 along the side of the waterway. Continue with a stream on your left through a rural industrial estate with a farm shop and café. Turn left just before a large warehouse to cross the stream and go through a field to a stile into woods by the M3 motorway. Turn right to a footbridge and cross to enter Bartley Heath nature reserve.
10.5 miles

10 BARTLEY HEATH

The next bit of route is tricky, but pylons provide a clue. One line of pylons crosses the motorway to the right of the footbridge, but soon afterwards divides, one line turning right and the other very slightly left. A well-marked track passes near

the pylon junction and heads along the right branch of pylons. Follow this track, but only for about 70 metres, and look for a narrow path to the left roughly halfway between the first and second pylon. The path at first runs roughly parallel and to the right of the left branch of pylons, which are half hidden by trees. Soon the path crosses a small bridge over a ditch. Continue and after some distance ignore a path to the right by a line of overhead cables. Walk on to reach the B3349 just to the right of a roundabout. At the roundabout turn right onto a road leading into Hook and signed to the station, which is less than quarter of a mile away.
11 miles

Margaret Dickinson, Lydia Syson, Liz Valentine, Maggie Jennings.

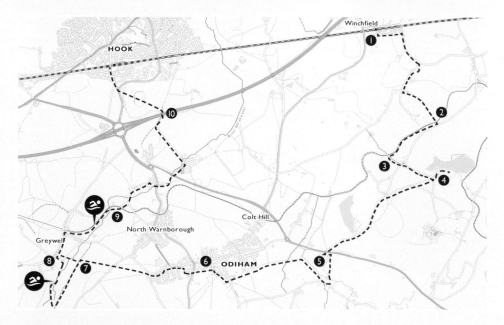

Walk 13

MARLOW CIRCULAR, BUCKINGHAMSHIRE

Two circular walks from Marlow, starting out over wooded hills in the Chilterns then dropping down to the Thames, with several opportunities for river swims.

T his walk sets off over wooded hills then drops down to follow the Thames. This is regatta country, homeland of all kinds of leisure boating from competitive rowing to genteel idling. The famous event is Henley Royal Regatta held around the beginning of July, but Marlow and other river towns have less formal regattas with a mixture of serious sport and family fun. This part of the Thames could be where Ratty in *The Wind in the Willows* coined the phrase 'messing about in boats' and it is certainly the setting for some of the adventures in the comic novel *Three Men in a Boat*. Sadly for swimmers, the motor launch dominates the waterway now, but you still see skiffs and dinghies and pass places where you can catch the smell of varnish and hear the squeak of rowlocks.

The first opportunity to swim is near Medmenham ❽, although the flow can be brisk. The lane leading down to the river ends at a slipway where there used to be a ferry. The service stopped running years ago, but the site is marked by a ceramic-tiled memorial, ironically celebrating a Parliamentary battle to make it a public service. This is a good spot for a picnic as the grass is mown and there are a few benches. Access to the water is relatively easy because the bank is reinforced with concrete, the water at the edge is quite shallow and the river bottom firm.

Aston ⓰ has beautiful water meadows with good swimming, down the lane by the Flower Pot Hotel, and Hurley has a popular beach at the far east end of the island, behind the locks. Another good place to swim is near the end of the walk opposite Bisham Abbey ⓬ where the river is calm, deep and still.

INFORMATION

DISTANCE: Marlow Circular 11 miles; Marlow Extended Circular 16 miles.

TIME: Marlow Circular 5 hours; Marlow Extended Circular 7.5 hours.

MAP: OS Landranger 175 (Reading & Windsor); OS Explorer 172 (Chiltern Hills East) and, for Marlow Extended Circular, OS Explorer 171 (Chiltern Hills West).

START / END POINT: Marlow Station

PUBLIC TRANSPORT: Train from Paddington; change at Maidenhead (hourly service at time of writing).

SWIMMING: River Thames.

PLACES OF INTEREST: Marlow's old streets and riverside; World War 1 training trenches Davenport Wood; Medmenham Iron Age fort and St Peter and St Paul church; Homefield Wood nature reserve; Bisham Abbey

REFRESHMENTS: Marlow for shops, cafes, pubs and restaurants. Extended Circular: The Flower Pot Hotel, Aston (RG9 3DG, tel 01491 574721).

WEEKEND SUGGESTION: Follow Extended Circular as far as Hambleden Weir but, after crossing the Thames, follow well marked Thames Path to stay in Henley. Next day take a train one stop or walk on the Thames Path to Shiplake and do the Shiplake Circular (walk 14). Swiss Farm camping (RG9 2HY, tel 01491 573419). Hurley Riverside Park (SL6 5NN, tel 01628 824493) is a good base for swimming and has tents in place for hire.

Marlow is an old market town, which probably developed because of its bridge over the Thames, a timber version of which existed by 1290. It has some attractive 17th and 18th century houses and famous visitors include Percy Bysshe Shelley, who stayed there with Mary Shelley in 1817 while writing *The Revolt of Islam*. To arrive by train you change in Maidenhead onto a charming branch line nicknamed the Marlow Donkey, probably after the type of engine used in the time of steam trains.

Both versions of the walk begin by heading out of the town into the chalk hills ❷-❺ where buzzards and red kites mew and soar on the thermals. On the way up we saw purple and white violets in March and a mass of poppies in June. Homefield Wood ❺, a nature reserve, is a good place for orchids and butterflies at the right time of year. You may see deer there and also in the woods dropping down towards Medmenham.

Historic sites include the remains of Bisham Abbey near the end of the walk ❿, World War I training trenches in Davenport Woods ❹ and an Iron Age hill fort above Medmenham, its ramparts forming the steep bank on the left of the lane leading to the village. The church of St Peter and St Paul in Medmenham ❽ has a Saxon foundation, was rebuilt in the 12th century, expanded in the 15th, and extensively restored in the 19th.

The Marlow Circular passes a weir ❿ where you can see the only surviving capstan wheel on the Thames. They were used to winch boats upstream, and this one, which has recently been restored, dates from 1300 and was preserved by Viscount Devonport, its 20th century owner. The Extended Circular takes in Hambleden Lock ❶❺ where it crosses the river by a long, narrow footbridge with beautiful views of the old mill buildings and the weir.

DIRECTIONS

Both walks
❶ MARLOW
From Marlow station walk in the direction the train was travelling to a nearby road junction and take Station Road, the second left, passing a pub called The Marlow Donkey on your left. Ignoring side turnings, go past the car park of The Prince of Wales on the left, and a rather grand town house, Marlow Place, on the right. Go on to Marlow High Street where you can see Marlow Bridge away to the left. Cross and go straight on

along Pound Lane, ignoring side turnings, to reach Henley Road (the A4155).
1.25 miles

❷ INTO THE HILLS
Cross Henley Road and take a small turning opposite (almost straight on but slightly to the left) and after 50 metres turn onto a waymarked FP on the right. Follow it between fences across a field heading slightly uphill to a wood. Pass a building on the left and continue alongside a plantation of young deciduous trees.

❸ When you reach Davenport Wood, a beautiful beech wood, follow waymarks for the Shakespeare Way and later also the Chiltern Way. Take care as there are a lot of side paths. Continue to a narrow road.
2.5 miles

❹ THROUGH THE WOODS
If you followed the correct path you will see on the other side a sign about WWI training trenches. If not, walk up or down to find the sign, then cross and go roughly straight on, taking care again as

DIRECTIONS

there are several tracks. A white sign on a tree indicates the direction along a rather faint path, which heads steeply downhill through the wood to a field, where it starts to go gently uphill and becomes a narrow fenced path beside a field. Go over a stile and turn left to cross the valley, ignoring a cross path, and continue until you reach a small road.
3.25 miles

❺ HOMEFIELD WOOD
Turn right onto the road and very soon turn left onto a signed path through Forestry Commission Homefield Wood, a nature reserve. Continue in a slight valley with trees each side. Turn left at the first waymarked cross path, marked with white arrows, leaving the Chiltern Way. Follow the path up a wooded bank, steep in places. At the top leave the woodland and join a track passing a house (Flint Cottage) on the right to reach a small road. Turn right and very soon turn left onto a marked FP with a stile.
4.75 miles

❻ DOWN TO THE VALLEY
Go over the stile and keep to the left-hand side of the field. On reaching a kissing gate, join a crossing path, bearing right towards farm buildings. Pass through a kissing gate in a fence, to the left of the farm buildings, and continue through two stiles in quick succession to the farm drive. Continue through the farm buildings, passing the farmhouse on the right. Go through a gate on the right to cross a very large field. The path is faint but a few clues suggest its route – the posts of a former gate and a small

single post. The best guide is a line of telegraph wires. Pass underneath and walk parallel to them, keeping them well to your right heading towards a gate on the far side.

❼ Go over a waymarked stile to the left of the gate. The path is supposed to cut across the corner of the next field bearing left, but if you cannot see it go round the edge turning left after the stile, then right at the corner, to follow the field edge to a waymarked stile leading onto a quiet road, Bockmer Lane.
6 miles

❽ MEDMENHAM AND THE RIVERSIDE
Turn right on the road and follow it down under beautiful beech trees for about half a mile to Medmenham on the main A4155 with a former pub (The Dog & Badger, now closed) on the right and a church opposite. Cross the main road and take the quiet road on the left of the church to reach the river at an abandoned ferry crossing. This is a good place to swim and to picnic and is where the Extended Circular diverges.
7 miles

Marlow Circular
❾ FROM MEDMENHAM
Retrace your steps towards Medmenham and, just before a little bridge, turn right onto a signed path, narrow and partly fenced. Follow it through kissing gates, with a stream on the left and houses on the right, to a meadow where you bear half right and pass through more kissing gates to a lodge on the far side. Go through the lodge gate and turn left onto a track to the main road.
7.5 miles

❿ HURLEY WEIR AND HARLEYFORD
Turn right onto the road and almost at once take a track off to the right, which passes through a wood then runs parallel to the Thames, but fenced off from it. Listen and look out for kingfishers here. There are chalk cliffs on the left. Soon you pass Hurley Weir capstan wheel.

⓫ The path leaves the river, rises and passes through a tunnel. At a path junction with a gate on the right, bear sharp right keeping the fence on your right. Enter Harleyford Golf Course (on your left). Continue, past Home Farm on the right, to the club house. Follow the FP signs, cross a driveway and take a FP downhill, cross another drive and you soon reach a meadow, across which you can see the river below on your right. You may also glimpse Harleyford Manor behind you to the right. Continue to a junction at East Lodge, where you take a lane to the right to pass Lower Grounds Farm with an outbuilding on staddle stones, which were originally used as supporting bases for granaries, hayricks, and game larders. This brings you back to the river where you join the route of the Extended Circular.
9 miles

⓬ TO BISHAM ABBEY
Turn left to follow the river path. After 5 or 10 minutes you will see buildings on the far side of the river which include the remains of Bisham Abbey. Around here there are possible entry points for another swim. Further down there is a good view of Bisham church on the far bank.

⑬ MARLOW

Follow the path into Marlow. At Marlow Bridge turn off the river path, go up to the bridge, turn left and shortly turn right onto Station Road to return to the station.
11 miles

Marlow Extended Circular

⑭ FROM MEDMENHAM RIVERSIDE

Go upstream along the Thames Path, keeping close to the river – there are more possible places to swim here. Still beside the river, go through a wooden gate into a field. From here there is no access to the river. Follow the edge of the field keeping the hedge on your left and go through a metal kissing gate to join a narrow, tarmac track. When the track bends right to reach a main road at Mill End, take a small path straight on to a driveway and turn right to the road. Turn left along the road to reach a FP on the left to Hambleden Weir.
9 miles

⑮ HAMBLEDEN WEIR

Cross the river by a long bridge and turn left downstream on a metalled track that soon veers away from the river. Follow it slightly uphill looking for a FP to the left that takes you onto a narrow road at the hamlet of Aston. (Alternatively, if you want to swim leave the metalled path to stay beside the river then walk up the road to Aston.)
9.5 miles

⑯ CULHAM COURT

Turn right up the road to pass The Flower Pot Hotel on your right then turn left on a waymarked FP (the Thames Path) just before the drive to Culham Court. Pass the walled grounds to join a track leading past another house on your right, then join a narrow road and pass a house on the left. Take a signed FP left through an iron wicket gate, down to the river and along the bank through a pleasant meadow. A second swim is tempting, but access to the river is impeded first by undergrowth and then by moored boats. At Medmenham Ferry,

opposite the earlier swimming place, swimming is possible.

⑰ A little further down the river there is a good view of Danesfield House standing on a chalk cliff on the far bank. Continue to Hurley Riverside Park, a caravan and chalet park where there is an open grassy area by the river and another swimming opportunity.
12.75 miles

⑱ HURLEY

Near Hurley there is a complex set of weirs where the river splits into different channels around islands. The path crosses one channel, crosses back again, passes a huge marina, enters a wood then crosses the river onto the north bank, where there is another weir and moored boats. Just after the weir where a path joins from the left, you rejoin the Marlow Circular.
14 miles
Then follow Marlow Circular, steps 12 & 13, for a total distance of 16 miles.

Margaret Dickinson, Clarissa Dorner, Liz Valentine.

Walk 14

SHIPLAKE CIRCULAR, OXFORDSHIRE

A varied walk starting along the Thames Path, where there are several places to swim, and returning over farmland with extensive views of the Thames Valley.

This is a lovely walk along the Thames Path from Shiplake to Sonning and back through contrasting scenery. There are several good swimming places along the Thames here. The first is just after you join the river, but be careful of passing boats in summer. Another good place out of term time is a little further on opposite Shiplake College Rowing Club ❶. There is no privacy for changing, beyond that offered by some bushes and mature trees.

The area around Shiplake has been cultivated since at least Saxon times, with strips of land rising from the river through meadows to woodland on higher ground. Binfield Heath, as the name intimates, was poorer land with common grazing rights. It is thought that the Vikings came up river as far as Shiplake. In more recent times, settlement has been determined by the creation of Shiplake Lock by the Thames Water Commission in 1773, and Shiplake station on the branch line (now known as the Regatta Line) from Twyford to Henley in 1857. Wargrave and Shiplake hold an annual regatta, the largest on the Thames after Henley. Shiplake featured in Jerome K Jerome's novel *Three Men in a Boat* and George Orwell spent some of his childhood here.

Sonning Bridge ❸, built in 1775, contains a curiosity in the form of a postbox between two arches of the bridge, which appears to be a folly. 'B|O' at the centre of the bridge marks the border between Berkshire and Oxfordshire, formerly that between Wessex and Mercia. Binfield Heath Non-conformist chapel ❺ was built of Bath stone in the Gothic Revival style in 1835, but it was closed on the two occasions we passed. (There is, however, a public toilet here, which was open.) Shiplake church ❻, dedicated to St Peter

INFORMATION

DISTANCE: 7 miles.
TIME: 4 hours.
MAP: OS Landranger 179 (Reading & Windsor) or OS Explorer 171 (Chiltern Hills West).
START POINT: Shiplake station.
END POINT: Shiplake station.
PUBLIC TRANSPORT: Train from Paddington; change at Twyford for Henley branch line. Free parking at Shiplake station.
SWIMMING: In the Thames between Shiplake and Sonning.
PLACES OF INTEREST: Sonning Bridge, Binfield Heath church, Shiplake Copse, Shiplake church.
REFRESHMENTS: The Flowing Spring pub near Dunsden (RG4 9RB tel 0118 969 9878); The Plowden Arms, Shiplake (RG9 4BX, tel 0118 940 2794); The Baskerville, Lower Shiplake (RG9 3NY, tel 0118 940 3332).
WEEKEND SUGGESTION: Combine with walk 13, Marlow Circulars (see this for details).

and St Paul, was also locked when we visited. It contains French 15th-century stained glass but was much restored in 1869 – its main claim to fame is that the poet Alfred, Lord Tennyson married Emily Sellwood here in 1850.

Shiplake Copse is noted for bluebells in spring. In August red kites, swallows and house martins wheeled overhead; Peacock, Speckled Wood, Small Whites and even a Brimstone butterfly fluttered amongst the flowers, while brown Hawker dragonflies and pretty blue damselflies skimmed over the water. The wild flowers, beginning to fade, still made a spectacular display bordering the Thames Path: greater common willow herb, Himalayan balsam, purple loosestrife, meadowsweet, hedge cranesbill, dock, angelica and marsh fleawort.

DIRECTIONS

❶ STATION TO RIVER

Turn left from Shiplake station then left into Mill Road – there is no pavement. Continue past Lashbrook Mead (on the left). Continue on the road ahead (note Thames Cottage, Baskerville Lodge, Appletree Cottage). Turn left at Lashbrook House, signed for the Thames Path (TP), right over the bridge and through two kissing gates to a small road. Turn right here (TP sign) and soon left (signed FP to Shiplake Lock and road sign TP to Sonning), through a kissing gate (right) to a meadow and path.

Arrive at the River Thames and note the weir after a few yards. Pass through another kissing gate. This is the first swimming spot. Continue over a wooden bridge, which can be muddy. Arrive at Shiplake College Rowing Club, another possible swimming place, and observe the beautiful flow of the River Thames.

1 mile

❷ THE THAMES PATH

Follow the river for about two miles to Sonning Bridge.

3 miles

❸ LEAVING THE RIVER

Walk up to the road and turn right along the pavement to reach the French Horn Hotel, a very smart country hotel with restaurant and beautiful gardens. There is a lovely picnic spot with a bench opposite the hotel at the river's edge beside a car park. Leaving the river, take a walled tarmac path past Furleigh Cottages. Turn left at a small road, passing an ancient brick and timber barn (on your left). Continue past The Homestead, ignoring a sign to Reading Sailing Club. Pass Dunsden Lodge, through a gate to a busy

road. Cross this road (B478) into Pool Spring Lane opposite.

3.25 miles

❹ TO BINFIELD HEATH

At the 'No entry' sign at the beginning of the road go through a gate on the right onto a footpath with allotments on your right. Continue parallel to the road through two fields and into a third, from which you turn left to rejoin the road. Turn right onto the road and note The Flowing Spring pub on your left. The pub has a casual and relaxed atmosphere with a garden, benches and homemade food (including gluten-free and dairy-free). At the junction with another busy road (A4155), cross and go up steps to a permissive path. Turn right into a field with a hedge on your right, then take steps down to a fence (FP sign on fence). Turn left, then follow the blue arrow uphill along a fenced bridleway, with lovely views. At a crossing track (red brick Bints Farm is visible to the left), keep straight on along a slightly sunken path to reach the road ahead opposite Dragon Cottage. You have arrived at Binfield Heath.

4.5 miles

❺ SHIPLAKE COPSE AND SHIPLAKE CHURCH

Turn right and pass Binfield Heath church. Follow the road past a letterbox (on the right) and turn right into a field (FP signed Shiplake 1½ miles). Turn right along two fields – there are open views across the Thames Valley to Berkshire. In the far corner of the second field,

bear right a few paces over a stile to enter Shiplake Copse and walk down through woodland. On emerging, follow a yellow arrow guiding left to the next field. There is a lovely view as you follow the path right. Keep left to another field defined at a marked stile. (If in doubt, follow the general direction.) Cross a field to a white cottage. Turn right at the road (Plough Lane) and continue to the main road (A4155), with the Plowden Arms on your right. Cross and go up Church Lane opposite, signed to Shiplake church.

6 miles

❻ BACK ALONG THE RIVER

Leave the church by the front (south) gate and take the path downhill (signed public bridleway). Continue downhill and turn left at a junction. You return to the river and Shiplake College boat yard. Turn left and retrace your steps, following the Thames Path sign. At a gate by the bridge turn left then turn right at the road, past a 'Restricted byway only' sign. Turn left at the TP sign, over the bridge, right onto the lane, and back to the station.

7 miles

Olga Way, Liz Valentine.

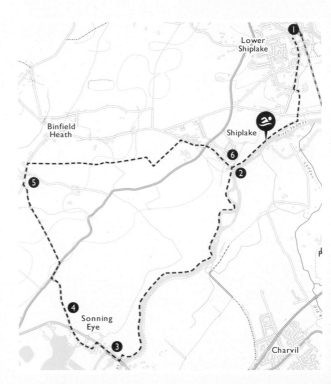

GORING AND STREATLEY TO CHOLSEY, BERKSHIRE

An easy walk through lovely surroundings
with a choice of many good swimming places.

T his is a glorious walk embracing wide stretches
of the Thames, open meadows, woody paths and
a beautiful Brunel railway bridge. With three
swimming spots, you can take your time in good
weather, enjoying a peaceful meander along the Thames Path
with views of the Chilterns.

The villages of Goring ❶ and Streatley ❷ have not always
been linked. The first bridge between them was built in 1837,
and a toll was charged until 1923 when the new bridge replaced
the old rickety one. Charges were based on numbers of sheep,
cattle and wheels on any vehicle 'propelled by steam, electricity
or anything other than horsepower'. The two settlements had
quite different histories, but both were affected by the coming
of the railway which destroyed the river trade.

St Mary's church in Streatley features in the Domesday Book
and was originally Saxon. It was rebuilt in 1300 and again by the
Victorians so not many original features remain, but the interior
is interesting for its striped pillars and Elizabethan brasses.

We did this walk in early September on a glorious day, had three
swims and spent time lounging in the open meadows and drinking
tea at The Beetle and Wedge riverside restaurant-café ❺. Without
such long breaks you could do the walk easily in an afternoon.

This is an easy route to follow because it hugs the banks of
the Thames for most of the way and is signposted as part of
the Thames Path. The path leaves the river at Moulsford, but
otherwise, the walk is uncomplicated and you can dawdle and
dream without worrying about getting lost. When the river is
running fast, take care and stay close to the bank. In normal
conditions it flows steadily and slowly and the swimming is
very enjoyable.

INFORMATION

DISTANCE: 4 miles.
TIME: 2 hours.
MAP: OS Landranger 174 (Newbury
& Wantage) and Landranger 175
(Reading & Windsor); OS Explorer
171 (Chiltern Hills West) and
Explorer 170 (Abingdon, Wantage &
Vale of White Horse)
START POINT: Goring and
Streatley Station.
END POINT: Cholsey Station.
PUBLIC TRANSPORT: Train from
Paddington to Goring and Streatley.
Return from Cholsey.
SWIMMING: The Thames.
PLACES OF INTEREST: St Mary's
church, Streatley; Isambard Kingdom
Brunel railway bridge, Moulsford.
REFRESHMENTS: The Swan pub,
Streatley (RG8 9HR, tel 01491
878800); The Beetle and Wedge
Boathouse, Moulsford (OX10 9JF,
tel 01491 651381).
WEEKEND SUGGESTION:
Combine this walk with walk 16,
Shillingford to Didcot. Instead of
turning off to go to Cholsey station
continue on the Thames Path either
2.5 miles to Wallingford or 3.5 miles
to Benson. Places to stay include The
Coachmakers Arms (OX10 0EU, tel
01491 832231), The George (OX10
0BS, tel 01491 836665) and The
Partridge Inn (OX10 0ET, tel 01491
839305) in Wallingford, and The
Crown Inn in Benson (OX10 6RP, tel
01491 838247). Next day continue
on the Thames Path to Shillingford
Bridge, about 1 mile on from Benson,
where you join the Shillingford to
Didcot walk.

DIRECTIONS

❶ GORING

When you alight at Goring, mount the steps and cross to the left hand side of the pedestrian bridge and along a path that follows the tracks for a few yards and turns into Station Road. (If you find yourself in a car park, you are the wrong side of the tracks!) Station Road takes you past thatched cottages and a community hall to a small opening

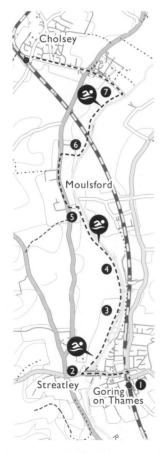

on the right, which leads through a tiny shopping mall onto Goring High Street where you turn left. Follow the road as it bears to the right, past Pierreponts café on the right and Goring Mill on the left, and soon you reach Goring Lock and the weir on the river.

❷ STREATLEY

Cross the bridge and turn right just past The Swan pub to St Mary's church. Exit the churchyard and follow the path alongside The Swan car park. Take a right fork for the Thames Path, which passes through a wooded area and across a field, onto the towpath, where you turn left and follow the river. We swam just after the path meets the river, just beyond a gate opposite a large property on the far bank with extensive lawns reaching down to the river. Look for a small clearing in the reeds where you can get in the water.

❸ Continue to Cleeve Lock which has a picnic tables and toilets.
1.5 miles

❹ UP RIVER FROM CLEEVE LOCK

The walk now opens out onto beautiful wide meadows with the Chiltern Hills to your left. There are a couple of swimming spots along this stretch and it is a good place to sunbathe on a hot summer's day. You will also see a pub on the opposite bank. The story goes that there was a farmer who would regularly swim across for a pint and swim back to return home. It's a tempting thought on a hot day.
2.5 miles

❺ MOULSFORD

You pass a more built-up area on your left to arrive at The Beetle and Wedge at Moulsford, which serves meals and teas. There is a pleasant outside area directly next to the water. On leaving, the path diverts away from the river and goes along the road. Follow the Thames Path signs and turn right to return to the river after passing Willow Court Lane on the left.
3 miles

❻ TO FERRY LANE

As the path returns to the river, you can see the Brunel viaduct ahead of you. When you pass beneath it you can wonder at the beauty of the massive arches and crenellated stonework. Follow the river path to the Ferry Lane turning on your left. About 100 metres past Ferry Lane, we found our third swimming spot at a small clearing under a willow tree.

❼ TO CHOLSEY

Retrace the path to Ferry Lane and follow it straight, crossing over a main road. Cholsey station is right at the end on the left, on Papist Way. It is a small station with no facilities, so it's worth knowing the train times in winter. In summer you can sit in the evening sun and look out over the fields while you wait for the train, which passes back through Goring on its return to London.
4 miles

Sarah Saunders.

Walk 16

SHILLINGFORD TO DIDCOT, OXFORDSHIRE

An easy walk with plenty of opportunities to swim in the River Thames, and optional visits to an Iron Age hill fort and a medieval abbey.

O n this walk you are never far from the Thames until the final stretch into Didcot. The going is easy, on flat land or gentle inclines, with constant views along the river or down towards it from slightly higher ground.

There are many possible swimming places – the river is quite wide and deep and easy to swim across. There is some river traffic, which you need to look out for, and there are several weirs, so avoid swimming too close to one. We had our first swim a little upstream from Shillingford Bridge Hotel, our second upstream from Day's Lock and our last just where the route leaves the river for the last time. In fact, there are plenty of swimming spots all along the river upstream from Day's Lock ❹-❺, although in some places the bank is steep and in others the river is shallow at the edge, but it is easy enough to paddle out to deep water.

In the earlier part of the walk a relative absence of recent development allows the landscape to evoke its long human history. There are Roman and pre-Roman earthworks and a pattern of small villages on ancient sites. Most of them trace their origin back to Saxon times or earlier. Pottery excavated from the Sinodun Hills – site of a hill fort, crowned by the oldest planted hilltop beeches in England and also known as the Wittenham Clumps – indicates occupation from the first to the fifth centuries.

Little Wittenham is a tiny hamlet consisting of a few houses and the church of Saint Peter. The tower is 14th to 15th century but the nave was rebuilt in the 19th century. The main point of interest is an alabaster monument to Sir William Dunch, MP for Wallingford in the late 16th century, his wife (who was an aunt of Oliver Cromwell) and his children.

INFORMATION

DISTANCE: 8.5 miles.
TIME: 4.5 hours.
MAP: OS Landranger 164 (Oxford) or OS Explorer 170 (Abingdon, Wantage & Vale of White Horse).
START POINT: Shillingford bus stop by The Kingfisher Inn, Shillingford.
END POINT: Didcot Station.
PUBLIC TRANSPORT: By train from Paddington to Reading; bus X39 or X40 from stop EB outside Reading Station to Shillingford (buses run by Thames Travel, tel 01865 785400). Return by train from Didcot.
SWIMMING: River Thames.
PLACES OF INTEREST: Little Wittenham weirs; the Wittenham Clumps and Iron Age hill fort; St Mary's church and Pendon Museum, Long Wittenham; optional visit to Dorchester on Thames which has a medieval abbey and museum.
REFRESHMENTS: The Kingfisher Inn (OX10 7EL, tel 01865 858595) and Shillingford Bridge Hotel (OX10 8LZ, tel 01865 858567) in Shillingford; The Plough Inn (OX14 4QH, tel 01865 407738) and Waggon & Horses (OX14 3BW, tel 01235 525012) in Long Wittenham; plenty of places in Dorchester on Thames, just off the route.
WEEKEND SUGGESTIONS: Break the walk in Dorchester on Thames; places to stay include The George Hotel (OX10 7HH) and Fleur de Lys Inn (OX10 7HH, tel 01865 340502). Alternatively, combine this walk with walk 15, Goring and Streatley to Cholsey (see this for details).

The village of Long Wittenham ❻ has a number of old houses, several with cruck frames, including a cottage alleged to date from the 13th century. The church dates from the 12th century and contains various Norman features: the chancel arch, a window in the north wall of the chancel and a remarkable round lead font decorated with bishops standing beneath an arcade, with rosettes and wheels above. It was hidden from Cromwellian soldiers and forgotten, then rediscovered in the 19th century. The font cover and other woodwork in the church is Jacobean; in the chancel there is a most unusual carved piscina. At the end of the village you will find the Pendon Museum with a collection of model railways and landscapes, housed in a former pub building.

DIRECTIONS

❶ SHILLIINGFORD BRIDGE
There are two bus stops in Shillingford. Alight at the second (by The Kingfisher Inn) at the west end of the village, retrace your steps to the crossroads and just beyond Wharf Road take a narrow, enclosed footpath signed for the Thames Path. After about 300 metres, at the bottom, bear left onto a minor road, which takes you to the main road, where you turn right to cross over the Thames by an attractive bridge. Just after the bridge turn right along the river bank where there

is a lawn belonging to Shillingford Bridge Hotel, which charges £15 for picnicking on its lawn. So, don't have your picnic here.
0.5 miles

❷ TO LITTLE WITTENHAM WOOD
Beyond the hotel lawn keep to the riverside footpath (note, this is not the Thames Path) where there are possible places to swim as the path soon leaves the river. At first the bank is high and overgrown but soon there are spots where you can enter the water through

reeds. The path leaves the river by a kissing gate (there is another good place to swim just beyond this) and heads off along the edge of a field with a ditch and hedge on your left. At a junction of paths, turn right on a bridleway which runs into a farm track. (Taking this track to pass North Farm on your left would be the shortest route, but does not appear to be a right of way and the bridleway makes a loop below the farm.) Follow the bridleway as it veers off left to pass North Farm on your right, crossing

another farm track. At a path T-junction turn right then left to rejoin the track from the farm. Continue on this bridleway to reach Little Wittenham Wood. This is the only significant wood on the walk, which may be useful to bear in mind if it is very hot or pouring with rain.

1.5 miles

❸ OPTIONAL DETOURS AND A SHORTCUT

Follow the path through the wood, which leads straight on and slightly uphill.

Detour 1: Just before leaving the wood turn left to visit the Iron Age fort on Castle Hill (Wittenham Clumps), from where there is a spectacular view over the Thames valley – a perfect place for a picnic. From here descend by a footpath to Little Wittenham to rejoin the main route. (This adds about one mile.) If you do not make the detour, continue straight on to emerge on the far side of the wood at a meadow where there are beautiful views, across the river below and up to Wittenham Clumps. Follow the path gently downhill to a lane where you turn right into Little Wittenham. Go past the church and continue to cross three bridges, the last two over the Thames. On the far side there are three paths, one that turns sharp left, one that bears left, and the Thames Path that bears right along the river back to Shillingford. *Detour 2:* Take the path that bears left to the fairly large ancient village of Dorchester on Thames, where there is an abbey

church, a museum and a pub. Explore and return to where you crossed the Thames. (This adds about two miles.)

Optional shortcut: If you do not want another swim, you can take a direct byroad from Little Wittenham to Long Wittenham. In this case retrace your steps over the bridges (if you crossed them) back past Little Wittenham church and continue on the lane to turn right at a junction, taking a minor road and cycleway to Long Wittenham. (This saves about 1.5 miles.)

Main route: From the last of the bridges take the sharp left path to follow the river bank to Day's Lock and a weir, where you cross back over the river and turn right to follow the river path upstream.

As soon as you are far enough from the weir you can swim. *Continuing mileages are for the route with neither detours nor shortcut.*

2.5 miles

❹ BESIDE THE THAMES

Follow the Thames Path by the river for about two miles through open meadows with little shade or shelter. After about a mile you start to see scattered buildings on the far bank, boat houses, a few old villas and some rather dull, modern houses. Shortly after the buildings finish, look for a path leading away from the river to Long Wittenham. It is not easy to spot because there is no noticeable turning, the sign is inconspicuous and, when we did the walk, it appeared to point into a

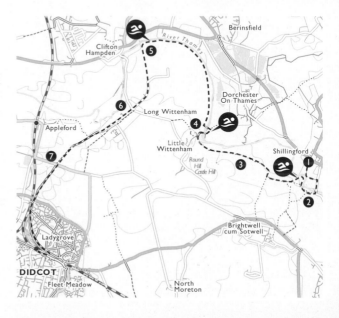

dense bed of reeds. When we parted the reeds, however, we found there was a boardwalk in perfectly good repair. (If you miss the path you reach a road a quarter of a mile upstream and can turn left there to Long Wittenham, but look out for traffic.)
4.5 miles

❺ TO LONG WITTENHAM
Assuming you find it, turn left on the path, which soon becomes a pleasant grassy track lined with bushes. After a little over half a mile it comes to a junction with a hard track where you turn right and soon pass some buildings on your right. Keep to the lane, which veers slightly left then straightens out and continues to

Long Wittenham, passing a few outlying houses on the right.
5.5 miles

❻ TOWARDS DIDCOT
Long Wittenham lives up to its name as it lines the road for nearly a mile. As you come in there is a crossroads where you carry straight on, down the main street. (This is where the shortcut rejoins the route.) The church of St Mary's is at this end of the village. In the middle of the village the main road turns left but continue on the minor road ahead, which is a cycle route (NCR5). At the far end of the settlement is the Pendon Museum. From here, stay on the cycle route, which soon becomes

an off-road track and heads across flat fields to Didcot.
7 miles

❼ DIDCOT
The cycle track crosses a main road and continues through fields to the edge of Didcot where it goes under the ring road. A short distance after passing under the bypass, where the cycle track is signed to the left, continue on the footpath straight ahead. Soon it runs beside the main railway. Eventually, you reach a road where you turn right under the railway and then right again to arrive at Didcot station.
8.5 miles

Margaret Dickinson, Liz Valentine.

A WALK AROUND PORT MEADOW, OXFORD

A gentle stroll around the historic water meadows that inspired Alice in Wonderland, and back along the Thames Path to Oxford.

T his walk, on a lovely May morning, is a paradise of wild flowers, bird life and history. The path out of town runs along the Oxford Canal, lined with narrowboats, and offers a view of the Italianate square tower of St Barnabas church. It calls to mind John Betjeman's *Myfanwy at Oxford* with the line 'Tubular bells of tall St Barnabas'.

Port Meadow, grazed by cows and horses for 1,000 years and mentioned in the Domesday Book, is a lovely expanse of land running beside the Thames, flooded when the river is high and blazing with buttercups and white hawthorn blossom in the late spring. The grazing rights now belong to the commoners of Wolvercote, the charming little village at the north end of the Meadow. This is the setting and inspiration for the opening lines of *Alice in Wonderland* when Alice was 'beginning to get very tired of sitting with her sister on the bank' and the closing lines where Alice sees 'an ancient city and a quiet river winding near it along the plain'.

Beside the meadow is a nature park, created several decades ago by Oxford City on the site of a vast rubbish dump. On a recent visit a young red kite tried to hover, unsuccessfully, and a skylark rose from the grass.

Wolvercote is home to several good pubs, and a bridge takes the walker over the Thames to head back into town along the Thames Path, past the site of Godstow Abbey ❹. Rosamund Clifford, a famous beauty (known as Fair Rosamund) and mistress of Henry II, was buried there when she died circa 1176. The nuns of Godstow seem frequently to have got up to mischief with the young men of Oxford – how many students must have undertaken the walk out to Godstow in the abbey's medieval heyday!

INFORMATION

DISTANCE: 6 miles.
TIME: 3 hours.
MAP: OS Landranger 164 (Oxford); OS Explorer 180 (Oxford).
START POINT: Oxford Station. Alternatively, the bus station at Gloucester Green, about a quarter of a mile east of the railway station.
END POINT: Oxford Station, or Wolvercote and return to central Oxford by bus.
PUBLIC TRANSPORT: Train from Paddington; Oxford Tube, a fast coach service from Victoria Coach Station.
SWIMMING: River Thames.
PLACES OF INTEREST: Ruin of Godstow Abbey, Wolvercote.
REFRESHMENTS: The Anchor (OX2 6TT, tel 01865 510282) and The Trout (OX2 8PN, tel 01865 510930) at Wolvercote; The Perch (OX2 0NG, tel 01865 728891) and countless eateries in Oxford.

Along the river there are lots of wonderful bathing spots, with a gently shelving grassy shore, although we found little cover to change behind, save a few clumps of hawthorn and bramble. The Thames here is relatively clean and shallow at the edges.

Iris Murdoch, who was a big outdoor swimmer, wrote in a piece in the New York Review of Books in March 1993: 'On hot days in the Oxford summer, my husband and I usually manage to slip into the Thames a mile or two above Oxford, where the hay in the water meadows is still owned and cut on the medieval strip system. The art is to draw no attention to oneself but to cruise quietly by the reeds like a water rat: seeing and unseen from that angle, one can hear the sedge warblers' mysterious little melodies, and sometimes a cuckoo flies cuckooing over our heads, or a kingfisher flashes past.' This sounds like a spot just north of Wolvercote, but the drifting method works well in the meadow too.

DIRECTIONS

❶ OXFORD CANAL

Turn left immediately on leaving the main entrance of the station and follow signs to the Oxford Canal. Take the green cycle path between the station car park and the Said Business School. The path swings to the right after about 100 metres. Shortly after, turn left down Stable Close, across Rewley Road, and along Rickyard Close to the canal. Turn left along the canal, crossing the Rewley Road bridge, then turn right along the footpath and over a narrow pedestrian bridge to join the canal. Walk north (left) along the canal path, admiring St Barnabas on the far side the canal on the right. At Bridge 240 (all the canal bridges are numbered) come up to road level, and turn left past the recreation ground (if you want to visit The Anchor, follow Aristotle Lane eastward). Head east along Navigation Lane and take the continuation along a dirt path over a railway bridge.
1.9 miles

❷ PORT MEADOW

Emerge onto a concrete path running north south along Port Meadow. Instead of following it, turn right through the gate into Burgess Field Nature Park and follow the gritted track. After 0.9 miles it splits: take the left fork through a metal gate over a wooden bridge.

2.8 miles

❸ WOLVERCOTE COMMON

You now leave the nature park and are at the part of the meadow known as Wolvercote Common. Ahead is a row of houses: cross the open ground over the low bridge, heading towards the houses at the right end of the row. If you want to end the walk now, go through the Jubilee Gate onto a road where there is a bus stop for the number 6 bus, which will take you back to central Oxford. However, to continue the walk, turn left across the common, skirting the houses and admiring the views of Cumnor Hill. Aim for a small wooden gate between a car park and a thatched cottage, which will let you out onto the road.

2.9 miles

❹ GODSTOW ABBEY

Go along the road, crossing a narrow bridge and passing The Trout. A second bridge takes you to a gate on the left side of the road, which leads to the Thames Path. This is where the path passes the ruins of Godstow Abbey and Godstow Lock. The next mile of riverside offers the best swimming spots – and a turn-off to The Perch inn. This is a long stretch of riverside walk, lovely on a fine day.

4.76 miles

❺ FROM BLOSSOM'S BOATYARD

At Blossom's Boatyard, you have a view of an Oxford University planning mistake: graduate housing near the railway called Castle Mill, jutting up over the trees. Turn left over the arched metal bridge, walk another 200 metres along the stream then cross a second metal bridge to the left to return to the main stretch of Port Meadow. The middle of three paths from the bridge heads back to the concrete strip and the entrance to the path by the nature park, which takes you back to the canal.

5.35 miles

❻ TO THE STATION

Follow the canal path back to the railway station. There is an M&S and several food shops in the station, for a hungry swimmer to recover before catching the train home.

6 miles

Frances Cairncross

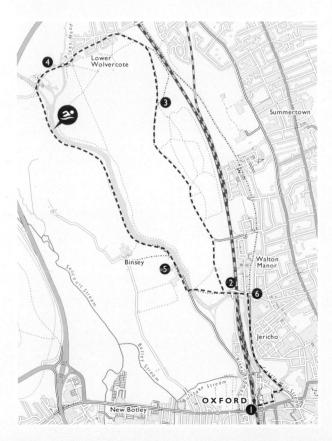

Sea

To the northeast, east and south the sea is not far from London, and the resort boom of the 19th century bequeathed a dense network of railways linking the capital to the coast.

This means there are plenty of sea walks to choose from, despite extensive development: we selected ours based on the quality of the swimming and for a variety of landscapes, significant landmarks and historical interest. Some parts of our routes, like the cliff tops on the way to Deal and the wooded foreshore above Covehurst Bay near Hastings, are so unspoilt and little frequented that it is hard to believe London is just over an hour away.

The geology of the South East makes for a coastline with few deep indentations or rocky outcrops. From the London basin soft clays and grits stretch northwards to form the low-lying foreshore of Essex with its long, straight beaches. The coast to the south is more varied due to the two great chalk ridges which plunge dramatically into the sea, the North Downs at Dover and the South Downs at Eastbourne. The celebrated white cliffs can be seen on the walks near Dover and Seaford.

Many beaches in the South East are shingle and, although hard on bare feet, they have advantages in that picnics remain sand-free and the sea tends to be clear. One of the best swims in the book is from the shingle beach of Cuckmere Haven. Sandy beaches, granted, are in many ways more inviting and almost half our swims are off sand – Leigh, Frinton, Margate, Broadstairs and Folkestone.

Some of the maritime towns that our walks include are historically important. By the 12th century five ports along the Kent and Sussex coast had formed a confederation known as the Cinque Ports, and over the next 400 years a series of Royal Charters granted them privileges in return for providing ships for military use. The confederation added two Ancient Towns and a varying number of other ports of which eight remain, designated as 'limbs' of the original five. Our walks visit two of the Cinque Ports, Hastings and Dover; both the Ancient Towns, Rye and Winchelsea; and three limbs, Deal, Folkestone and Margate. Invasion remained a recurrent threat along the coast and the walks between these towns pass many reminders of the danger, from medieval castles to the Martello towers of the Napoleonic Wars to World War II gun emplacements.

In the 19th century ports and fishing villages began to reinvent themselves as elegant resorts, then in the 20th century expanded to embrace mass tourism, only to decline when tourists defected to sunnier destinations. Traces from all these phases colour the different walks. Leigh, with its cockle processing and views of distant industry, has something of the energy and mess of a working port, as does the busy ferry terminal in Dover. The Leas area of Folkestone exudes a leisurely elegance, while in Margate tasteful terraces hide behind a brash commercial front, both sharing an air of having seen better days. Some of these towns are experimenting with regeneration strategies, including the promotion of contemporary art. Margate has the new Turner Gallery, Hastings has the Jerwood and Folkestone runs the popular Triennial, when artists are invited to create new works in public spaces.

One drawback of the coast near London is that the resort boom began so early that much of the seaside was lined by straggling development before planning regulations or the National Trust became effective. As far as possible, our walks avoid such sprawl, either by approaching the sea from inland, or by taking advantage of the few remaining gaps.

Walk 18

KIRBY CROSS TO FRINTON AND WALTON-ON-THE-NAZE, ESSEX

A perfect summer's walk both inland across countryside and through two contrasting seaside resorts, with sea swims from sandy beaches.

*U*ntil late Victorian times, Frinton-on-Sea was nothing more than a church, several farms and a few cottages. It may be hard to picture this now, but the first part of the walk gives a sense of what it might have been like. From Kirby Cross station ❶ a little white gate opens directly into fields and, apart from a short stretch of road, footpaths lead through open countryside, past the village of Great Holland, all the way to the sea. A huge sea wall now forms a dramatic barrier, but beyond it the sandy shoreline remains remarkably deserted.

In the 1890s, suggestions for a pier in Frinton were rebuffed by the town developer, and pubs and boarding houses were also prohibited. By the first half of the 20th century the resort attracted high society with its lido, palm trees and first-class hotels. Now, times have changed again and, although boasting nothing more than a small high street and one pub, the quiet and natural charm of Frinton draws ever-growing numbers of swimmers, sun worshippers and nature lovers. With its beautiful sea front, sandy beach and jauntily painted beach huts, it is easy to find your own entertainment here in the peace of this quintessentially English seaside town. You will find yourself back in a world of cheese and tomato sandwiches, knotted handkerchiefs, striped deckchairs and Thermos flasks of tea – there are no ice-cream stalls or fast food vans, and it is heaven. Carry on walking along the front until you reach the pier, and you are then in Walton-on-the-Naze. The atmosphere here is a quite dramatic change from the serenity of Frinton, with pubs, chip shops and the pier itself.

All the way along the shore, from the rural stretch through the resorts, the swimming is exceptional. The beaches are sandy and pleasant for sitting on at low tide, with breakwaters in the resorts

INFORMATION

DISTANCE: 10.5 miles (options of 7.5 and 5 miles).
TIME: 5 to 6 hours for full walk.
MAP: OS Landranger 169 (Ipswich & The Naze); OS Explorer 184 (Colchester, Harwich & Clacton-on-Sea).
START POINT: Kirby Cross Station (or Frinton Station for short option).
END POINT: Walton-on-the-Naze Station.
PUBLIC TRANSPORT: Train from Liverpool Street, usually change at Thorpe-le-Soken. The train stops frequently and can be boarded at Stratford or stations further east.
SWIMMING: In the North Sea.
PLACES OF INTEREST: All Saints church, Great Holland (Thomas Hardy, as a young architect, assisted with the restoration); sea defences at Sandy Point; Frinton sea front; the Naze nature reserve and cliffs; the Naze Tower.
REFRESHMENTS: The Ship Inn, Great Holland (CO13 0JP, tel 01255 674809); numerous cafés and pubs in Walton-on-the-Naze including a café at the Naze Tower (CO14 8LE, tel 01255 852519).
WEEKEND SUGGESTION: Divide the walk in two by staying in Walton-on-the-Naze so that you can linger on the lovely beaches and explore the Naze at leisure.

every 100 metres or so that also act as windbreaks. In Frinton there is a wide grassy area overlooking the sea that provides a place to sit at high tide.

Swimming is possible at most stages of the tide. On one visit we swam at low tide and, after a bit of paddling, were soon able to swim in waters which gradually deepened and changed colour from sandy brown to a delicate, pale turquoise. At high tide the water can reach the sea wall and even moderate waves could make swimming dangerous. We found it tricky getting into the water at very high tide due to quite excitable wave action, but it was nothing any confident swimmer couldn't handle. Generally, the extent of shallow water and absence of currents make the beaches very welcoming for children and weak swimmers.

Just north of Walton-on-the-Naze is the John Weston Nature Reserve ❺, a great place to spot a wide variety of sea birds. The shoreline rises here to form low cliffs famous for fossils, and it is a dramatic example of sea erosion. At the southern end, a viewing platform was recently constructed at sea level, from which you can see the layers of rock that form the cliffs: London Clay, Red Crag and gravels. Threatened by the approaching sea is the 86-foot Naze Tower built in 1720 as a navigational mark to aid shipping. It now houses an art gallery, a museum of the Tower, a tea room and a roof-top viewing platform with spectacular views of Essex, Suffolk and, on a clear day, Kent. From the cliffs the land slopes down westwards to the salt marshes and backwaters where, if you are lucky, you might spot harbour seals or grey seals ❺.

The Naze is a well-loved open space and especially important for wildlife conservation because it contains several distinct habitats: heathland, woodland, salt marsh and cliffs. Yet it only survives as it is because local people successfully resisted plans in the 1960s to develop it into a massive holiday camp. Large areas were bulldozed flat in preparation, so that the trees there now were nearly all planted since 1968, after the development was halted. Perhaps, if the conflict were happening now, the local objectors would be decried as Nimbys.

DIRECTIONS

❶ FROM KIRBY CROSS
At Kirby Cross station cross the railway tracks at the pedestrian level crossing at the east end of the platform and go straight ahead through a small white gate leading to a hard surfaced footpath through a field. On reaching a road, the B1032, turn right along it ignoring a signed footpath to the right. The road is busy but there is a pavement. Take the first turning to the left then, after the first house on the right, take a signed but slightly overgrown footpath over a stile on the right. As the path approaches the far side of the field, follow the waymarks right then left to go through some trees to a minor road. At the road turn left, or for the pub in Great Holland, which is about quarter of a mile off the route, turn right.
1 mile

❷ GREAT HOLLAND TO THE SEA
Pass the church of All Saints', Great Holland, on your left. Pass the Hall, also on the left, where

the road becomes more of a track. Just before a duck pond turn off right and soon, when the track forks, take the right-hand branch leading across open land towards the distant sea. About a quarter of a mile further on the track turns right, but take a signed footpath straight on. A little further on a track turns right but again keep on the footpath straight on. Cross a golf course, where the path is marked by low black and white posts, and continue to the sea defences where steps leads to a beach the other side, a good place for a first swim.

2 miles

❸ FRINTON AND WALTON-ON-THE-NAZE

Turn left and walk either along the top of the sea defences or, depending on the tide, along the beach to Frinton. Here there is a choice between walking on the promenade by the beach huts or on the cliff top to enjoy the sea views. Sandy Hook breakwater is a small landmark about halfway. Continue along the front until you reach Walton-on-the-Naze pier.

5 miles

❹ THE NAZE

The station is just inland from here, but unless you want to cut the walk short, carry on along the promenade to approach the Naze Tower –to visit it, take a path up from the car park. The Naze is a nature reserve where you can wander around freely. To complete our walk, head to the tip of the Naze either along the cliff

tops or below along the Crag Walk, a newly constructed track, or, if the tide is out, along the beach. The cliffs continue to the tip of the Naze where they drop to near sea level, and the beach and cliff top routes meet.

7 miles

❺ THE NAZE BACKWATERS

Walk on round and back via the backwaters along a dyke built to protect the low-lying land. It runs west, then turns south by the Walton Channel and eventually leads to Walton. The path comes out on a road by a fish and chip shop and café. Turn right here and walk down the road to the sea front. Turn right and retrace

your earlier steps to the pier. Just before the pier, turn right uphill and continue up to a brick building, which was once the station; just past it is the much smaller modern station.

10.5 miles

SHORTER OPTIONS

Shorten by 7.5 miles by staying on the train to Frinton Station, then head down Connaught Avenue to the Esplanade, where you join our main route at Frinton sea front. Shorten by 5 miles at Walton pier – head inland straight to Walton-on-the-Naze station instead of walking around the Naze.

Bryony Fane, Margaret Dickinson

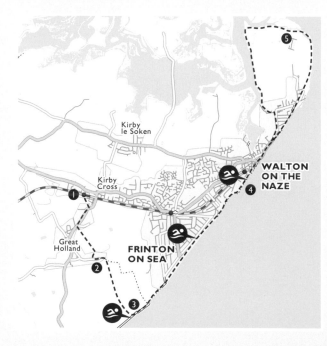

Walk 19

BENFLEET AND LEIGH-ON-SEA, ESSEX

This walk takes in a tidal creek, a ridge-top castle and a seafood extravaganza in a lively fishing village, plus swims in the Thames Estuary.

*T*his walk picks its way fastidiously through the heavily industrialised Thames Estuary. Despite never being far from a power station or oil refinery, the route benefits from the particular peace that comes from tidal waters, whether you're watching moored boats gently bobbing in the current, or the uncanny transformation when water turns to mud and boats are stranded at unexpected angles. The return leg of the walk takes you back centuries in your imagination, visiting the remains of a castle on a stretch of untouched hillside.

The swim is dependent on the tide and the variants of the main route are suggested not only for different lengths, but to help you plan your arrival at Leigh beach when the tide is right, preferably not more than two hours before or after high tide.

From Benfleet station you find in front of you Benfleet Creek (Hadleigh Ray on some maps), a tidal stream connecting to the Thames. Our walk takes you along the creek, passing many boats, some of them houseboats. The path follows the top of a high dyke created to prevent flooding. The salt marsh below it features assorted flotsam and jetsam; we saw small, dried-up crabs. A little way along, you could divert across Two Tree Island, now a nature reserve and an important stopping-off point for migrating birds.

The creek opens to the Thames Estuary at Leigh-on-Sea. You walk past some large cockle sheds, traditional home of the cockle trade, and the working dock ❸. Old Leigh is a single street lined with fishermen's cottages, pubs, restaurants, shellfish stands and a gallery or two. It is picturesque but also still a working fishing port. This, and the throngs of people out enjoying themselves, makes the atmosphere special. It feels far from London but, in an odd way,

INFORMATION

DISTANCE: 8.25 miles for Benfleet Circular (options of 4, 5 and 5.25 miles).

TIME: 5 hours (2, 3 and 3.5 hours for options).

MAP: OS Landranger 178 (The Thames Estuary); OS Explorer 175 (Southend-on-Sea & Basildon).

START POINT: Benfleet Station (Leigh Station for optional route).

END POINT: Benfleet Station (Leigh or Chalkwell Station for optional route).

PUBLIC TRANSPORT: Train from Fenchurch Street, London.

SWIMMING: In the Thames Estuary at Leigh-on-Sea.

PLACES OF INTEREST: The old cockle sheds and two excellent fish and seafood stalls (perhaps consider bringing a cool box), art gallery, restored fisherman's cottage in the heritage centre, all in Leigh-on-Sea; ruins of medieval Hadleigh Castle; views of Olympic mountain biking track.

REFRESHMENTS: The Crooked Billet (SS9 2EP, tel 01702 480289) and The Peterboat (SS9 2EN, tel 01702 475666) plus bars, cafés and seafood stalls in Leigh-on-Sea; Salvation Army Tea Room at Hadleigh Farm (SS7 2AP, tel 01702 426268).

part of it – a slice of old East End culture, cockles, whelks and all, transported to the seaside.

At the end of this so-called High Street – the real high street is up the hill and called the Broadway – is the children's beach. For a conventional swim, time your arrival close to high tide so you can swim from the sand. We swam about three hours after high tide and had to wade out a long way, but the mud underfoot was firm and not unpleasant. Some lads were jumping off the dock into deep water. Low tide has its own attractions. We stayed for a while and the scene when the tide had retreated was alone worth the walk.

All that was left of the sea was a narrow channel, with mud flats and eelgrass beds stretching out into the estuary. Children and teenagers were swimming in the waist-deep channel or sliding on their bellies down mud slopes into the water. The mud flats have deep channels carved within them and there was something primeval in seeing mud-covered children disappearing and reappearing, apparently from the mud. If you are tempted to try a bit of mud larking yourself, there are showers at the sea end of the toilets so you can restore a somewhat civilised appearance before leaving the beach.

The return route to Benfleet is via Hadleigh Castle. The path starts next to Leigh-on-Sea station and very quickly you are in fields. As you start to climb, you get a different perspective on the Thames Estuary, with refineries and power stations appearing and the occasional large ship, if you're lucky. The walk is fairly flat until you come to a gate in the hedge and an idyllic grass path leads up towards the castle ❻. For a moment modern life disappears – you might catch a glimpse of a knight sleeping under one of the little oak trees. As you walk up the grassy ridge the two end towers of the castle come into view, one leaning in a Pisa-esque fashion. A last scramble and you are within the walls of the castle, which was enlarged by Edward III to protect the estuary from attack by France. At that time, before the building of flood defences, the water would have lapped the ridge the castle stands on.

This is a fantastic castle to explore: a single information board, walls you can climb, and a sign stating that the opening hours are 'Any reasonable time'. We're still puzzling over what would be an unreasonable time…

Next to the castle is the site of the 2012 Olympic mountain biking event. The track is due to open for public use in 2015. The castle tea room and surrounding farmland is owned, surprisingly, by the Salvation Army. Originally the Army ran the site as a 'colony' where destitute men from London were sent to do character-building work before being sent home or to the real colonies to work. The farm later became an establishment for 'juvenile delinquents' before making a final transformation into today's tea room and rare breeds farm, which are run as training projects for people with 'barriers to employment'. The café is a bit gloomy and institutional inside but the tables on the terrace have a lovely view of the farm and the distant estuary. From the castle it's a peaceful walk down the hill and through fields back to Benfleet.

❶ BENFLEET

Leave the station through the exit to the right by the ticket office. Benfleet Creek is on the other side of the road. Don't cross the road but turn left on the road and follow it to the corner where the road turns right to cross the creek. Take the path ahead passing the flood barrier on your right. Pass Benfleet Moorings. Follow the path along the dyke, with the creek on your right.

2 miles

❷ BENFLEET CREEK

Where Benfleet Creek divides, the path tracks the smaller of the two branches, north of Two Tree Island. Cross a road and then a path. Take the lower of two paths, between the bank and the water. (For Two Tree Island turn right on the road and follow footpath signs once on the island.)

3.15 miles

❸ INTO LEIGH-ON-SEA

The path joins a road, passing Leigh-on-Sea station on the left, and curves round Leigh Marina. Follow the road past the green cockle

sheds. Walk along High Street until you come to the sandy beach and the swim spot. Alternatively, turn right after Osborne's and walk along the sea front until you have to return to the High Street.

3.75 miles

❹ OUT OF LEIGH-ON-SEA

To see more of Leigh-on-Sea, from the beach take the footbridge over the railway line, turn right up the hill, then left up Church Hill. Retrace your steps to the station. To continue our walk back to Benfleet, pass the station on the north side and walk past a taxi rank and through a car park. At the end of the car park, walk across the grass to pick up the marked path, along Castle Drive, on the far side. Walk to the end of the tarmac.

4.75 miles

❺ TO HADLEIGH CASTLE

Take the footpath that heads off to the right round the field. Follow the path as it winds gently up then gently down until you reach a gate on your right in the hedge. Go through and up the grassy path. At

the top, go through the green kissing gate and turn left to climb up to the two towers of the castle.

5.75 miles

❻ HADLEIGH COUNTRY PARK

Leave the castle by the gate at the back. Follow the stony track ahead if you want to visit the tea room and farm. Otherwise, turn left through the gate and follow the track down the hill towards the Thames. Just before the bottom there is a grass path going diagonally right to a kissing gate. This leads to the gravel track/cycle path. After a while cross a cattle grid into Hadleigh Castle Country Park. Before a second grid leave the cycle path and walk straight on, taking the grassy path across the field then running along the hedge on your right.

(For the Leigh Circular, the path crossing the railway branches off south just after the first cattle grid.)

7 miles

❼ BACK TO BENFLEET

The path gradually converges on the railway line and you will begin

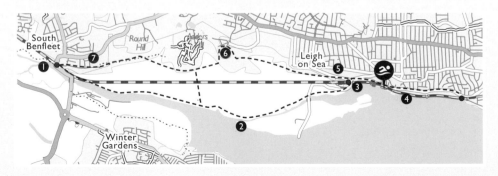

to see landmarks you passed at the start of your walk. Follow the bridleway, which is signed, until it narrows to a path between two high hedges, then a wider gravel path. Come out in Station Road with a view of the estuary. Turn left and walk down to Benfleet Station.
8.25 miles

Route options

Benfleet to Leigh (4 miles): Follow step 1 then after about 1.5 miles, before the creek divides, look for a track on the left leading to a gate to a level crossing over the railway. Cross the railway and walk to a T-junction where you turn right. Refer to steps 5 and 6, but in reverse, to guide you to Hadleigh Castle and then Leigh-on-Sea, where you can catch the train home.
Benfleet to Chalkwell (5.25 miles): As above, but continue walking from Leigh-on-Sea between the sea and the railway to Chalkwell, the next station along the line.
Leigh Circular (5 miles): Stay on the train to Leigh-on-Sea station. Follow directions from step 4 to 6, but after the first cattle grid look for the path on the left crossing the railway (the same path as for Benfleet to Leigh, above, but from the other direction). Take this and continue to the embankment by the creek then turn left to return to Leigh along the creek, following steps 2 and 3.

Ros Bayley, Maggie Jennings, Clarissa Dorner.

149

Walk 20

MARGATE TO BROADSTAIRS, KENT

A coastal walk including the Turner Contemporary gallery, a glimpse of a historic lido and a swim in the renowned Walpole Bay sea pool.

From Margate, where JMW Turner spent his holidays, to Broadstairs, loved and frequented by Charles Dickens, this route offers the pleasures of these two seaside resorts. Decay and neglect are still evident along the route, but there are signs of renewal too.

The Turner Contemporary gallery ❷, opened in 2011, is part of a more general effort to tempt people to coastal resorts for art and culture. Dreamland Amusement Park, a grand attraction in the past, is to open its doors in 2015 for the first time in a more than a decade, after a campaign by local people to retain the site as a vintage theme park. The fire-damaged scenic railway will be restored and there are also plans to reinstate the 1930s cinema and bingo hall.

The future of the Cliftonville Lido ❹, a popular swimming venue until the seventies when it was damaged by a storm, is unknown. Many would like to see it restored, but the cost would be considerable. The steps to the pool end in a scrubby area of grass and sand, and the bright red lido tower is a sad reminder of past glory. The Walpole Bay sea pool ❺ is a treat for swimmers. Created in 1900, it gained Grade II listing in 2014, as one of the largest and most intact of the 13 tidal sea pools in England. It is hoped that this will lead to some restoration and attract more swimmers to this extraordinary site.

Leaving Margate towards Foreness Point, a number of lovely sandy coves appear at points beneath the cliffs. Botany Bay, flanked by empty low tide sands, is only reachable at low tide. The cliffs above contain impressive caves carved out by

INFORMATION

DISTANCE: 6.5 miles.
TIME: 3 hours.
MAP: OS Landranger 179 (Canterbury & East Kent); OS Explorer 150 (Canterbury & the Isle of Thanet).
START POINT: Margate Station.
END POINT: Broadstairs Station.
PUBLIC TRANSPORT: Train from Victoria Station or St Pancras International Station. The cheapest day tickets are from Victoria.
SWIMMING: In the North Sea.
PLACES OF INTEREST: Turner Contemporary gallery and The Lido, Margate; Dickens House Museum, Broadstairs.
REFRESHMENTS: Lots of pubs and cafés in Margate and Broadstairs; along the route places include a café at Jet Ski World, Palm Bay (CT9 3DF, tel 01843 231703), Botany Bay Hotel (CT10 3LG, tel 01843 868641), The Captain Digby, Kingsgate (CT10 3QH, tel 01843 867764) and Joss Bay Café (CT10 3PG, tel 01843 604073).

smugglers of the past. Beyond, a dramatic sight is Kingsgate Castle ❽, an extravaganza built in the 1760s by the infamously corrupt Henry Fox, Lord Holland. It was originally designed as a gothic folly to be viewed from Fox's main residence, Holland House, but was later adapted to become a stately home. Subsequent owners include Lord Northcliffe, proprietor of the *Daily Mail*. In the 1920s it was turned into a grand hotel and it is now luxury flats. The name Kingsgate was given to the nearby village by King Charles II after difficulties at sea caused him to make an unscheduled landing in the bay.

Finally, Joss Bay awaits, where a small surfing school runs during the summer, before the final stretch of the walk to Charles Dickens' Broadstairs, and the train home.

DIRECTIONS

❶ MARGATE BEACH

From Margate station, follow Station Approach and turn left onto a footpath that takes you to a crossing over the main road to the promenade. Your first swimming spot is here in the sandy bay next to the boating pool. Over to the far right facing seawards, you can see the Turner Contemporary gallery. Directly behind you, on the main coast road, is Dreamland. There are pubs, cafes and small shops to explore, and on a hot day the atmosphere is festive.
0.5 miles

❷ THE TURNER GALLERY

Make your way across the beach or along the promenade to the Turner Contemporary gallery. On the way, you may want to savour rollmops or cockles from the fish stand, or you can visit the gallery café. Entry to the gallery is free; it is well worth a visit.

❸ THANET COASTAL PATH

On leaving the gallery, pick up the Thanet Coastal Path, which you will follow for the rest of the walk. Depending on the tides, you can walk along the promenade or the sand.
1 mile

❹ THE LIDO

Go past the Winter Gardens and you will reach the Lido, a magnificent swimming area in its heyday and now an area of sand and grass bounded by a sea wall. It is shown on the map as a semicircular shape projecting onto the sand.
1.5 miles

❺ WALPOLE BAY SEA POOL

Walk on for about half a mile to the Walpole Bay sea pool, a walled pool that fills at high tide. It provides a wonderful swim, except around high tide when waves wash over the walls. Check the Walpole Bay Facebook page for suitable swimming times. After the pool continue for another mile.
3 miles

❻ BOTANY BAY

Follow the path to the end of Botany Bay, where a chunk of cliff stands separated from the mainland. There is a café on the beach at this point, where you can climb up the path onto the cliff top.

❼ NEPTUNE'S TOWER

On the cliff path you will pass Neptune's Tower, the ruin of a folly built by Henry Fox in the 18th century, one of several follies surrounding his Broadstairs home of Kingsgate Castle.

4 miles

⑧ KINGSGATE AND JOSS BAY

Further along the path you can see Kingsgate Castle across the bay from the Captain Digby pub. You can get to a beach café, the Joss Bay café, a little further down the road.

⑨ TURN INLAND

The path now follows the cliffs above the beach, before turning

left inland along the main road, the B2052, for half a mile. Look out for where the path resumes, a left turn into Park Road, drops down, and leads into town next to the beach, lined with colourful beach huts.

6 miles

⑩ BROADSTAIRS

In Broadstairs you can enjoy a last swim and enjoy fish and chips or a pint. If you have not dallied too much, as we did, you may even have time to visit the Dickens Museum. To reach the station turn inland near the Dickens House Museum and

take High Street, the B2052, or turn inland opposite the bandstand in Victoria Gardens and follow Oscar Road, York Avenue and Pierremont Avenue, turning right at the end to join High Street near the station.

6.5 miles

Sarah Saunders

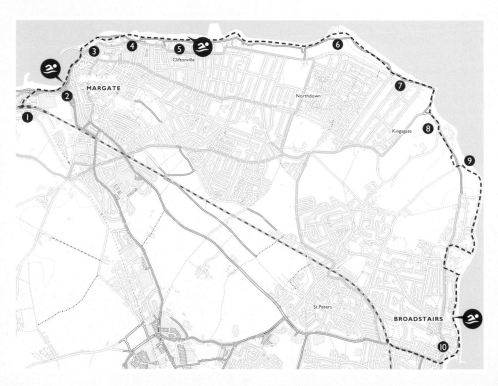

Walk 21

CANTERBURY TO SWALECLIFFE, KENT

A walk from the medieval city of Canterbury, through gentle countryside along part of the Crab and Winkle Way, and to the coast for a sea swim.

INFORMATION

DISTANCE: 8.5 miles (9.5 miles starting from Canterbury East Station).
TIME: 3.5 to 4 hours.
MAP: OS Explorer 150 (Canterbury & the Isle of Thanet); Landranger 179 (Canterbury & East Kent).
START POINT: Canterbury West Station or Canterbury East Station.
END POINT: Chestfield & Swalecliffe Station.
PUBLIC TRANSPORT: Southeastern Railways from Charing Cross or Southeastern Highspeed from St Pancras International (there is a surcharge) to Canterbury West; Southeastern from London Victoria to Canterbury East. Return from Chestfield & Swalecliffe station to London Victoria, or to St Pancras International by changing onto the Highspeed (with surcharge) at Faversham. It may be best to buy a return to Canterbury and a single from Chestfield & Swalecliffe to Faversham, where the routes join.
SWIMMING: In the North Sea at Swalecliffe or Tankerton.
PLACES OF INTEREST: Canterbury historic city; Blean church; Long Rock, Swalecliffe.
REFRESHMENTS: Plenty of pubs and restaurants in Canterbury; The Wheatsheaf Hungry Horse (CT5 2LU, tel 01227 792310), Plough Inn (CT5 2RN tel 01227 792428) and Mr Beano's Café Restaurant (CT5 2QT, tel 01227 374343) in Swalecliffe.

The walk starts from Canterbury, a historic city with city walls and many medieval houses, but above all famous for its cathedral, the mother church of the Anglican Communion, called in full the Cathedral and Metropolitical Church of Christ at Canterbury. In the Middle Ages, Canterbury was one of Europe's important pilgrimage destinations and from the 12th century, centre of the cult of St Thomas Becket, the archbishop who quarrelled with King Henry II, was murdered in 1170 and canonised in 1173. Now the cathedral and other ecclesiastical buildings nearby are a World Heritage Site and major tourist destination. The walk is too long to combine with serious sightseeing, but those arriving at Canterbury East will walk through the old town, passing near the cathedral, while the route from Canterbury West heads up a hillside from where there are impressive views of the cathedral below. The building as it appears now is mainly 12th century, although the foundation dates back to 597.

The walk climbs up through the grounds of the University of Kent, Canterbury and joins the Crab and Winkle Way ❷, a cycle route named after the disused railway, and a much older salt route along which salt was transported from Seasalter to Canterbury. The railway, opened in 1830 and soon nicknamed the Crab and Winkle Line, was the first anywhere to carry passengers on a regular basis. On the hilly parts of the line trains were hauled by cables powered by fixed steam engines, while steam locomotives hauled the rolling stock on flat stretches. There is an information board close to the entrance to Tyler Hill Tunnel, the first steam passenger railway tunnel, now home to bats.

The route passes the ancient village of Blean ❸ and a 13th century church, dedicated to Saints Cosmos and Damian, with a magnificent crown-post roof. The church's origins are older than the building, as it stands on the site of a Roman villa and a chapel here was mentioned in the Domesday Book. Listen and look out for skylarks on the field to the right and for other birds in the church-yard, and note the interesting information board here. After Blean the route goes past some of the orchards Kent is famous for, before plunging into Clowes Wood and on to Shrub Hill in Chestfield. It then descends into the village of Chestfield, crossing the major A299, and on to Swalecliffe for a well deserved swim in the sea.

This route was first walked on a gloomy day in November, when flocks of winter thrushes and herring gulls heralded the approach to the sea. There are good views on a clear day, and on a fine spring day in late April there were bluebells and stitchwort in the woods and plenty of warbler birdsong.

The North Kent seaside is quite built-up and our route from Canterbury reaches it in the middle of ribbon development stretching from Seasalter to Herne Bay. None of the possible ways through entirely avoids dull streets, but our route keeps them to a minimum. The seafront itself is very pleasant, with a wide promenade backed in some places by a grassy slope and in others by brightly painted beach huts. The swimming is good from the shingle beach between mid and high tide, but towards low tide the retreating sea exposes some estuarine mud.

Our walk directions end at Swalecliffe station, but an option is to walk on along the front to the old fishing village of Whitstable, which is famous for oysters and by far the prettiest of the adjacent seaside towns. Whitstable station is one stop on along the line from Swalecliffe.

DIRECTIONS

The route is written from Canterbury West station; alighting instead at Canterbury East enables you to walk through the city but will add a mile to the distances. From Canterbury East, cross the footbridge straight ahead on leaving the station. Turn right onto the city wall with Dane John Gardens to the left. At the end of the gardens, descend and turn left into Watling Street. At the second crossroads turn right into St Margaret Street. On reaching High Street, if you want to visit the cathedral go straight on along Mercury Lane, but otherwise turn left into High Street. Cross a river into St Peter's Street. Cross another river by West Gate, continue and turn right into Kirby's Lane. As it bends left (to Canterbury West station) continue straight on a footpath, joining our route from Canterbury West.

❶ CANTERBURY
From the main entrance of Canterbury West station, turn left into Station Road West, right into Kirby's Lane, and immediately left into a passageway between new houses, then left on a small road keeping parallel to the railway. There are brief views of the cathedral to your right. Cross two roads and pass under the railway. Follow signs for the cycle route to

the university. On reaching St Stephen's open area, turn left along its southern side, signposted for the university. Just after the green area, fork right (signed National Cycle Route 1) with houses on the left and a wooded bank on the right. Turn left at Beaconsfield Road and cross it on the pedestrian crossing. Take the

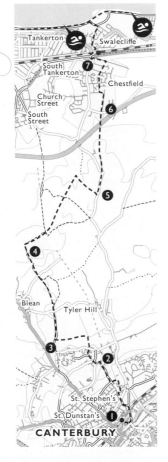

first right into St Michael's Road, signed for the cycle route to the university. Quite soon you can avoid the drab housing in this road by taking a path behind the houses on your right, on a wooded bank with playing fields to the right. This is actually the old Crab and Winkle railway line. After Tyler Hill Tunnel, turn left following a blue arrow for about 50 metres, then right (signed for the University and the Crab and Winkle Way link). Continue uphill through the university grounds with views of the cathedral below. Pass through the central university buildings, with the Students' Union building on your right.

1.25 miles

❷ THE CRAB AND WINKLE WAY

Bear right at the road, then left at the T-junction with a busier road, Giles Lane. Note Tanglewood, a weatherboarded house, on your left. Take a footpath to the right, signed for Park Wood. You pass the University Sports Centre on your right. At the next path junction turn right, leaving the Sports Centre on your right. There is a pond on your left. Pass between large buildings (the one on the left is called Jennison). At the end, cross the perimeter road and take a footpath opposite into Brotherhood Wood. Follow the yellow waymarks on posts and trees downhill, later crossing a stream. At the bottom, cross two footbridges and turn left, signed Blean Walk. Follow the field edge with the Sarre Penn stream on

your left, known locally as the Fishbourne. Cross another footbridge into a second field. At the far end of this, turn right onto a metalled track, marked by blue arrows. This is the Crab and Winkle Way (CWW).

2 miles

❸ BLEAN

Walk uphill to Blean church. After visiting the church, cross Tyler Hill Road (named after a medieval pottery and tiles industry). Keep left on the CWW and pass Arbele Farm on the left and Amery Court, a beautiful Georgian house, on the right.

3 miles

❹ TO CLOWES WOOD

Pass some farm sheds and after the track bears right, leave the CWW at a junction of fields, taking a right fork on an enclosed footpath between fields. Enter woodland (soon chestnuts on the left and conifers on the right) and continue straight on to a path crossing in a clearing (the CWW is visible to your left). Very soon after this take a left fork footpath off the main track. After crossing under the pylons, take an indistinct but signed right fork. Follow this path on through Clowes Wood, continuing straight on at a cross-path and later over a gravel track. Soon after this, on reaching a broad grassy path, turn right onto it. On reaching Radfall Road, by the Dog's House Rehoming Centre and opposite Mill Farm, turn left.

5 miles

❺ TO CHESTFIELD

This half-mile stretch of busy road is unavoidable but it is tree-lined and there is a verge to walk on. At the 30mph sign where the road bends left, continue straight on along Broomfield Gate, marked with a FP sign. At the end of the houses, pass through a kissing gate and continue on between bushes to the open grass of Chestfield Golf Course, with good views to the right. Soon you can hear the noise of the A299 and see the coast and outskirts of Chestfield. Follow the waymarks. At the cross-paths on Shrub Hill follow the sign for Molehill Road, taking a path downhill with a wood on your right, approaching the main road obliquely. (Do not bear left and head directly for the main road.) You pass two seats and cross the fairway to enter a small wood. Climb a short hill to cross the A299 by a most cleverly landscaped bridge. The road enters a tunnel just here and, but for the noise, you would not know it was there. Once over the other side, the noise soon subsides and you find yourself at the edge of Chestfield.

6.5 miles

❻ TO SWALECLIFFE.

Continue past houses on your left, crossing The Drove into a private road opposite with a right of way on foot. The golf course is on your left (on the far side you can see oast houses and the timber-framed clubhouse, claimed to be the oldest in the world) and houses are on your right. At the

crossroads in Chestfield village, turn left (signed for Swalecliffe) and follow the road round, passing a bizarre house (The Paddock) on your right. In a few yards, take a signed footpath on the right into Meadow Drive. Keep straight on through housing to a footpath between houses. There were sparrows chattering in the hedge here. Cross several more residential roads, finally turning left to emerge on the main road near a petrol station and a roundabout, where you turn left. Chestfield & Swalecliffe railway station is the far side of the roundabout.

7.5 miles

❼ TO THE SEA

To reach the coast, cross under the railway bridge. If you want the shops or a pub, turn left after the bridge and then right into Swalecliffe Court Drive. Otherwise, you can turn right after the bridge, take a FP on the

left just before the community centre, then right into Swalecliffe Court Drive. Follow it down, past the Victorian parish church of St John the Baptist with a steeple. At the end, turn left along the Oyster Bay Trail to reach the Saxon Shore Way. There is an information board here about Long Rock, the shingle spit straight ahead, which is a protected site noted for birds. However, a short distance to the left there is an area suitable for swimming with a row of beach huts and groynes. You may wish to continue west for just under a mile to the popular Tankerton beach. Alternatively, you can walk along to the right beyond Long Rock to a promenade and further swimming area, towards Herne Bay. Whichever you choose, retrace your route to return to the station.

8.5 miles

Liz Valentine, Cath Cinnamon.

161

Walk 22

DOVER TO DEAL, KENT

This walk begins at the beach where Channel swimmers depart, leads through flower-filled meadows over the famous white cliffs of Dover, and ends on an impressive shingle strand.

*E*njoy your first swim in Dover Harbour. Every year hundreds of Channel swimmers train here and then wait for favourable weather to attempt a crossing. Captain Matthew Webb made the first recorded Channel swim in 1875, taking 21 hours 45 minutes. Gertrude Ederle became the first woman to succeed in 1926 and broke the then record with a time of 14 hours 39 minutes. Now there is a constant stream of swimmers, 15 pilot boats and two organisations, the Channel Swimming and Piloting Federation and the Channel Swimming Association, that regulate, certify and advise swimmers. Even during the week you may catch sight of a Channel hopeful among the holidaymakers; we met Rohan More from Pune, India and Avram Iancu, who was hoping to be the first Romanian to complete the swim.

The Dover Museum has a small exhibition on Channel swimming. The White Horse pub in St James Street/Castle Hill is worth a visit: hundreds of successful swimmers have signed their names on the walls and ceiling. An evocative sculpture (On the Crest of a Wave 1995 by Ray Smith) on the seafront celebrates all the swimmers, while Matthew Webb has his own statue a little further east.

The past is vividly present in and around Dover. Priory Station ❶ is named after a 12th century monastery that was dissolved by Henry VIII. Dover College, a public school founded in 1871, took over and restored the remaining Priory buildings and the walk passes close to the flint-built refectory. A brief diversion takes you

INFORMATION

DISTANCE: 9.5 miles.
TIME: 5 hours.
MAP: OS Landranger 179 (Canterbury & East Kent); OS Explorer 138 (Dover, Folkestone & Hythe).
START POINT: Dover Priory Station.
END POINT: Deal Station.
PUBLIC TRANSPORT: Trains from St Pancras or Charing Cross.
SWIMMING: In the English Channel.
PLACES OF INTEREST: The Channel swimmers' training beach in Dover; South Foreland Lighthouse; The Pines Garden and Museum, St Margaret's at Cliffe; Dover, Walmer and Deal Castles; the Timeball Tower, Deal.
REFRESHMENTS: Numerous eateries in Dover. Along the route places include: National Trust café (CT15 6HP, tel 01304 852463), South Foreland lighthouse; The Pines Garden tea room (CT15 6DZ ,tel 01304 853173) and The Coastguard pub (CT15 6DY, tel 01304 851019), St Margaret's at Cliffe; The Zetland Arms (CT14 8AF, tel 01304 370114), Kingsdown; The King's Head (CT14 7AH, tel 01304 368194), Deal.
WEEKEND SUGGESTION: Combine this walk with Walk 23, Folkestone to Dover, starting in Folkestone and staying in Dover. Alternatively, just spend a day exploring Dover.

to the Roman Painted House, a house demolished by the Romans to make way for a new fort. The wall paintings that survived by a fluke are said to be the best in Britain, although it's not quite Pompeii.

Dover Castle towers over the town and thousands of years of history are contained within its walls. A little further on the ruined lighthouse was built by the Romans and there is a Saxon church. The site has been a fort from the Iron Age to 1958 and tunnels deep in the chalk were used from Napoleonic times until the Cold War.

The juxtaposition of the past and the present in Dover is sometimes quite brutal. You approach the Roman Painted House through the scrappiest of car parks. In Cannon Street the broad, five-storied west tower of the church of St Mary makes a striking contrast to the cafés, stores and charity shops. The balconied sea front houses at Marine Parade now look out over four lanes of container lorries straight off the ferries. Just behind is East Cliff, a street of small houses cowering under the great slabs of white chalk that rise steeply behind. Enjoy this view of the chalk from below: for most of the walk you will be fighting vertigo as you peer over the edge to glimpse it beneath you.

As you walk along the cliff top pay tribute to two great British institutions: our much-maligned planners and the National Trust. Between them, they have kept some stretches of coast free from creeping development. The best parts of the walk are on National Trust property where flower meadows in July were full of wild carrot, marjoram, viper's bugloss and ladies' bedstraw.

From the eyrie path you come to a wide natural amphitheatre ❸. In this apparently flawless landscape, it is surprising to read that an aerial walkway used to take coal down to the harbour from Tilmanstone Colliery seven miles inland.

Coming down into St Margaret's at Cliffe you may want to visit the beautiful Pines Garden and Museum, which has displays about the role this stretch of coast played in the two world wars.

The pebble beach between wooden groynes at St Margaret's offers the second swim of the day. The sea current runs strongly from left to right and the groynes were built to slow the shifting of the shingle. Swimming is best from mid to high tide – at low tide, rocks and seaweed-covered clay make it tricky. Beware of another danger: mobile phone signals are more easily received here from France than the UK, which can make your calls unexpectedly expensive.

Before ascending to the cliff tops again, walk along to see the white modernist houses and the pitched roof house, White Cliffs, beyond. This was once the exclusive hideaway of Noel Coward. Ian Fleming bought White Cliffs in 1951 and made it his weekend home for the decade when he wrote most of the James Bond books.

Once back on the cliffs, a slight diversion is required to visit the Obelisk ❺, which is a memorial to the Dover Patrol, part of the Royal Navy charged during the First World War with preventing German ships from reaching the Atlantic through the English Channel. After leaving the National Trust's Bockhill Farm, the view north along the long shingle beach to Deal is revealed. Your time in the rarefied world of the cliffs is over.

A fascinating coastline lies ahead. The sea has thrown up a vast bank of shingle and out to sea are the Goodwin Sands, a semi-submerged reef that protects the coast from the full force of the waves. These sands are the stuff of legend – and eccentric fact. From the 19th century to early this century, cricket was played on them during extreme tides when the sand was exposed. Along the shore there are boats pulled up on the shingle and wooden fishermen's huts. The hard path behind the beach passes a string of quirky houses that look as if they were designed for retired sea captains; some even have flagpoles. Beyond Kingsdown, the shingle has been colonised by evergreen Holm oaks, a strange sight but not one favoured by naturalists who brand them alien invaders. You can swim anywhere along this endless shingle strand, but beware of currents; also, there are no lifeguards.

At Walmer there is a wide green where an information board records that Julius Caesar landed here in 55BC. About 1,500 years later, Henry VIII, having divorced his wife Catherine of Aragon, feared the Catholic powers of Europe might attack so built three castles to protect the sheltered landings behind the Goodwin Sands. Only ruins remain of Sandown, but Walmer and Deal castles are still standing, open to the public and worth a visit: Deal for its military interest, Walmer for its gardens. On reaching Deal visit the Timeball Tower, which initially conveyed semaphore messages for an anti-smuggling force. In 1853 the tower was converted to drop a ball controlled by a telegraph signal from Greenwich at exactly 1pm each day, so ships could set their chronometers, needed for calculating longitude.

Deal itself is a delight: painted houses line the sea front. Take the last of your swims on the beach in front of Deal Castle, with the view bounded on one side by the pier and on the other by the cliffs of St Margaret's. On a warm sunny evening nothing could be more inviting than a pint on the green in front of the King's Arms – except perhaps fish and chips on the end of the pier.

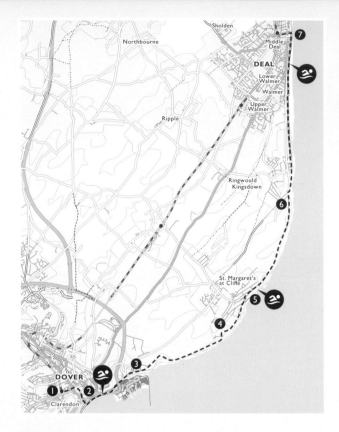

② DOVER BEACH AND CLIFFS

Emerge from the underpass, cross the circus with a statue in the middle and head for the Channel swimming sculpture on the sea front. Turn left and the last section of beach is the Channel swimmers' beach, with the Matthew Webb statue a little further on. This is the first possible swimming place. Walk along the sea front and, after the Premier Inn, cross by the traffic light, noticing the houses on Marine Parade. Go ahead and right into East Cliff. You are now on the Saxon Shore Way, which is intermittently waymarked all the way to Deal. At the end of East Cliff pass the terrace of white houses, then follow the path that gradually climbs up, with the chalk cliff on your left. The path goes under the A2. Take the right-hand flight of steps. At the kissing gate take the white chalk path to the right. Follow this path until it emerges into a grassy area with benches.
2 miles

③ ON THE CLIFF TOPS

Stray left to pick up a path that runs along the fence with a car park beyond. Pass the Visitor Centre. Continue on the white chalk path. Follow the pink National Trust signs round the green amphitheatre and continue along the coast path.
3 miles

④ TO ST MARGARET'S AT CLIFFE

The path leads up to the lighthouse then heads back towards the coast on a chalky white lane. Follow the Saxon Shore Way through a kissing gate on the right and walk through

① DOVER

Turn right out of Dover Priory station and follow the road until it joins Folkestone Road, B2011, where you continue ahead. Turn left into Effingham Street to see the priory refectory, now part of Dover College. Turn right into Saxon Street, noticing the well proportioned mid 19th century houses. Turn left at the end to reach the pedestrian crossing, then turn right towards the roundabout. Turn left into Priory Road, then right into Biggin Street, which becomes Cannon Street. Follow down to the market. Divert right down New Street if you want to visit the Painted Roman House. At the market square, cross diagonally left past the fountain. The museum is ahead to the right. Go ahead on King Street and down and through the underpass, noticing the tiles depicting ships that would have used Dover as a port through the ages.
1 mile

another flower-filled meadow, then out through a kissing gate. Follow the shady lane past the Pines Garden, bear right down to the beach at St Margaret's at Cliffe and right again at the road.
4 miles

⑤ CLIFF TOPS AGAIN

Look for the path that goes up from the beach quite near where you joined. At the top you may want to divert slightly to see the Dover Patrol Memorial. Keep following the path along the cliffs.
6.25 miles

⑥ KINGSDOWN TO DEAL

The path leads down to a road. Follow the road to Kingsdown (or walk on the shingle). Turn right along a line of houses culminating in the Zetland Arms. Follow the path in front of the houses facing the beach. Keep following this path all the way until it becomes a road shortly before Deal Pier, passing first Walmer then Deal Castles. For access to Walmer Castle, cross to the road parallel to the path just beyond the castle and take a side road into the grounds. For Deal Castle turn left into Marine Road, just before the castle, and cross the car park diagonally.
9 miles

⑦ DEAL PIER TO DEAL STATION

At the roundabout by the end of the pier turn left down Broad Street. This becomes King Street. Follow this road until you see Deal station on the right.
9.5 miles

Ros Bayley

Walk 23

FOLKESTONE TO DOVER, KENT

The day starts with swims from shingle coves or a sandy beach and continues with an airy walk over towering cliff tops and past mysterious relics of war.

There are so many good swimming opportunities around Folkestone that walkers may be tempted to change their plans and linger all day. This would be a mistake because, after an exhilarating climb, the walk offers spectacular views along a stretch of coast that has a special place in the history and mythology of Britain.

The nearby ports, including Folkestone and Dover, have always been the gateway to continental Europe and also the first line of defence in times of war. In good weather the coast of France, 21 miles away, is clearly visible and at night it is possible to pick out the lights of cars on the coast road. The chalk cliffs provide a dramatic greeting or poignant farewell to those travelling by boat, while the whiteness of the cliffs gave England its poetic name of Albion.

All along the route are reminders of this coast's role in defence: near the beginning and end are fortifications from the Napoleonic Wars, the Martello Towers near Folkestone ❸ and the Western Heights of Dover ❼, and in between are relics from the Second Word War and a Battle of Britain Memorial ❹ᵇ. A distant past is represented by views of the 12th century Dover Castle just before the descent into Dover.

Although the closeness to continental Europe could be dangerous in wartime, it brought wealth from trade and travellers. With railways came regular ferry services and Dover and Folkestone between them cornered most of the trade. They used to compete, with boats from Dover heading for Calais and those from Folkestone for Boulogne. Trains ran onto the quays and from Dover a special service, the Night Ferry, took first-class passengers onto the boat actually in their carriages, avoiding the struggle from

INFORMATION

DISTANCE: 9 miles.
TIME: 4.5 hours.
MAP: OS Landranger 179 (Canterbury & E Kent); OS Explorer 138 (Dover, Folkestone & Hythe).
START POINT: Folkestone Central.
END POINT: Dover Priory Station.
PUBLIC TRANSPORT: Fast, expensive trains from St Pancras or slow and only slightly less expensive ones from Charing Cross and Victoria. The Dover trains go through Folkestone so a day return to Dover will cover your travel.
SWIMMING: In the English Channel around Folkestone and the Warren.
PLACES OF INTEREST: Folkestone Leas gardens, harbour and warren; Battle of Britain Memorial at Capel le Ferne (10am to 4pm); acoustic mirror; Western Heights fort.
REFRESHMENTS: Pubs and cafes in Folkestone including The Mariner (tel 01303 254546) and The Ship Inn (tel 01303 251114) on the harbour. On route: Clifftop Café (CT18 7HP, tel 01303 255588), Capel-le-Ferne; The Lighthouse Inn (CT18 7HT, tel 01303 254080), on Old Dover Road, Capel-le-Ferne.
WEEKEND SUGGESTION: Combine this walk with Walk 22, Dover to Deal, starting in Folkestone and staying in Dover. Alternatively, just spend a day either in Folkestone or Dover. Folkestone Warren camping (CT19 6NQ, tel 01303 255093).

train to boat and boat to train. The journey used to take about eight hours, which makes the Eurostar feel like a magic carpet!

The Channel Tunnel, opened in 1994, passes under the coast between Dover and Folkestone to reach its Folkestone terminal. Ferry services from Dover survived, but Folkestone's gradually declined. The harbour railway closed in 1991 and a new hovercraft service, which replaced the ferry, finally closed in 2000, reputedly hit more by the end of duty-free shopping than by the tunnel. At the time of writing, the piers that carried the harbour railway remain a striking feature of Folkestone Harbour, but are scheduled for demolition – part of a redevelopment plan which has been intensely controversial.

The loss of the ferry followed the long decline of tourism and the town suffers from high unemployment and associated deprivation. There are, however, few signs of this on our walk, which starts in an area of large villas and hotels to reach the beautifully restored Leas Gardens that spread down the side of sloping cliffs. The way to the Lower Gardens is through the storybook caves and grottos of the Zig-Zag Path, built by the council in the 1920s to create jobs for the unemployed of that era. The other way down is by the Leas Lift, a Victorian grade II listed funicular railway at the eastern end of the gardens.

The first swimming opportunity is from Mermaid beach near Mill Point – it's a long shingly strand where little artificial bays have recently been created. The second swim is on the other side of Folkestone Harbour at Sunny Sands, a lovely sandy beach where swimming is nearly always possible, an exception being during a very high tide if waves are hitting the promenade. There are convenient alcoves under the promenade which provide some privacy for changing.

After Sunny Sands there are two options, both so good it may be hard to choose. One is to climb up to the cliff tops to join the North Downs Way, enjoy magnificent sea views and pass the Battle of Britain Memorial ❹ⓑ. The other is to enter the Warren, a Site of Special Scientific Interest created by repeated landslides. The railway line to Dover runs through it and is protected from storm damage by massive concrete sea defences. All along the shore, a mixture of sand, shingle and rocks, there are possible places to swim in calm weather, but underwater boulders and metal objects are a hazard. The route rejoins the cliff top one by taking a very steep, long, winding path up through woods to emerge at the Clifftop Café some way after the Battle of Britain Memorial.

The converged route continues along the cliffs past a strange structure, a great concave disc of concrete facing the ocean ❺. This is an acoustic mirror, a device used before radar to detect approaching aircraft, one of several built along the south coast before the Second World War.

A little further on our route turns inland, but walkers reluctant to leave the sea could ignore our directions and continue on the well-signposted North Downs Way into Dover. We offer the inland route partly because it leads very directly from green hilltops down to Dover Priory station and partly because it provides good, close views of the Western Heights fortifications ❼, as well as interesting, if disturbing, glimpses of Dover Immigration Detention Centre situated in the Citadel. From the point where our route bears inland, the coastal path loses some of its charm because of the proximity of the A20, although from the point of view of traffic noise there may be little to choose between the two.

DIRECTIONS

❶ FOLKESTONE AND THE LEAS

Leave the station and turn right and right again onto Castle Hill Avenue. At a roundabout go anti-clockwise and take the second right to stay on Castle Hill Avenue. Look for signs for the Hedgehog Route, a walk around Folkestone, which coincides with our route to the sea front. Keep going past side turnings and across two major junctions and along the last bit of road, called Langhorne Gardens on the left and Clifton Gardens on the right. Emerge onto the green space of the Leas by a statue of William Harvey. Cross to Leas Cliff Hall and the promenade along the cliff edge. Turn right to walk down (or left if you want to take the Leas Lift at a cost of £1 or 80p concession). Near the bandstand turn off onto the Zig-Zag Path to the Lower Leas Gardens and Mermaid beach, the first opportunity to swim.
0.75 miles

❷ LOWER LEAS AND THE HARBOUR

Turn left and walk through the Lower Leas Gardens or along the front, passing the back of Leas Cliff Hall. Go on to where the path joins Lower Sandgate Road at the foot of the Leas Lift. Walk along Lower Sandgate Road towards an isolated terrace, Marine Crescent. Either pass in front of the terrace on Marine Parade, to go past the old ferry terminal and round by the harbour, or branch left behind Marine Crescent and continue to join the Road of Remembrance where it sweeps downhill from the left and Marine Terrace turns off right. Go straight on past the Harbour Fish Bar to the harbour

and rejoin the Marine Parade route. Walk round the harbour under the old harbour railway (if it has not been demolished) and on past fish stalls, pubs and cafés to the end of the harbour, to arrive at Sunny Sands beach. This is the second opportunity to swim and, if you choose to take the cliff top route afterwards, it will be the last.
2 miles

❸ FROM SUNNY SANDS

On leaving the beach walk to the end of the promenade and up some steps. Veer right towards Harbour Church and take Wear Bay Road up the hill, passing a golf course and a white Martello tower on the right. Go on past a sports centre where there is a choice of route, down through the Warren or up to the cliffs.
2.5 miles

❹ THE WARREN

Just after the sports centre take a path on the right along a hedge towards the sea. At the end of the hedge, turn right and almost at once take a signed FP left down through bushes into the Warren, along a beach and onto concrete sea defences, which provide a rough promenade parallel to the Folkestone-Dover railway line. After about a mile, the chalk rock face briefly rises to tower above the promenade and then drops down to an area of bushy undercliff. Soon a track turns off left, inland, and just afterwards a path heads inland to a high pedestrian bridge over the railway. Take this path over the bridge and follow it as it climbs steeply, with many flights of steps, to pop out by the Clifftop Café.

❹ THE CLIFF PATH AND BATTLE OF BRITAIN MEMORIAL

Instead of turning right at the sports centre continue up Wear Bay Road towards a second Martello tower. Where the road bends slightly left, take a right turning straight on. At the tower the track turns right, but take a path straight on. Just before a bridge over a road the path divides and there are some waymarks. Keep straight on over the bridge and uphill. Near the top of a long climb there is T-junction where the path meets the North Downs Way (NDW). Turn right (unless you want to visit a pub, in which case turn left to The Valiant Sailor on the nearby B2011). The right branch of the NDW emerges on the cliff tops and after about half a mile passes the Battle of Britain Memorial. Shortly afterwards it drops steeply down and then up again to join a drive. Turn left on the drive and almost immediately the NDW continues on the right. Follow it to the Clifftop Café, where the cliff top and Warren routes join.
4.5 miles

❺ THE NORTH DOWNS WAY

Continue on the NDW parallel to the Old Dover Road. Pass The Light House Inn and follow the path as it turns away from the road and dips down a little to pass a chalet park on the left. (Nearby, on the road, there is another pub, The Royal Oak.) After the chalet park, pass a right turning signed to the Warren, but stay up on the NDW. Before a large white house the path forks and the NDW heads left, inland from the house, while a FP on the right follows the coast between the white house and cliff. Take either as they meet up after the house, where the NDW shares a route with a surfaced cycle track. Go down an incline to pass the acoustic mirror. Keep on the NDW when it diverges right from the cycle track. Soon afterwards it passes the remains of WWII defences and some large earthworks where young motorbikers sometimes noisily practise scrambling. After the mounds, pass a signed FP on the left and continue to a second FP on the left signed through a little gate, but hardly visible on the ground. This is where our route leaves the NDW but, if you prefer, you could continue on the well-signed NDW into Dover.

6 miles

➏ THE WESTERN HEIGHTS

Go through the little gate and aim for a similar gate on the far side of the field. The gate leads back onto the cycle track, now close to the A20 dual carriageway. Turn right and follow the cycle track for about a quarter of a mile to take a turning left through a tunnel under the A20. After the tunnel, the road forks; take the right fork. Pass a dead-end turning on the right and keep following the concrete road as it curves left, then turns right to go along the edge of a valley, dwindling to a narrow track overhung with bushes. The track dips down a little to a three-way junction where one path turns left, one heads straight on and one goes slightly to the right, uphill. Take the last one slightly uphill, a path with few vestiges of hard surfacing. It soon joins a surfaced track where you could turn right but instead keep straight on. You are approaching the Western Heights, a huge fort from the time of Napoleon. Pass some ruined military installations. When the path forks, keep to the right-hand upper branch. Soon you can see the citadel of the fort, which now houses Dover Immigration Detention Centre. The first houses of Dover are visible below on the left.

8 miles

➐ INTO DOVER

Continue on the path with the fort on the right. Keep up along the edge of the dramatic fortifications and deep dry ditches until you reach a road, the North Military Road. Just down to the left, take a signed FP to the left and follow it downhill. Near houses, take a turning to the right that leads past houses onto Clarendon Place, where you turn right and follow it down to the Folkestone Road (B2011). Turn right and the station is on the left down a flight of steps.

9 miles

Margaret Dickinson, Ros Bayley.

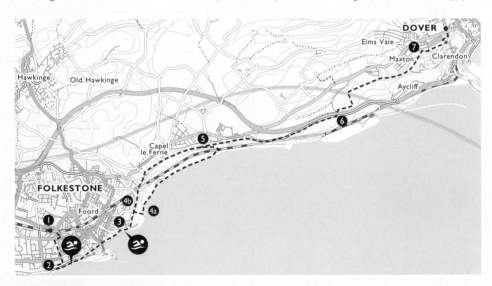

WINCHELSEA TO RYE, EAST SUSSEX

An unashamedly romantic walk through the remnants of an ancient, half-abandoned town, across desolate marshes, past a ruined castle to the coast.

few hundred years ago the site of Winchelsea station was under the sea. From a boat above it you would have seen the great, walled town of Winchelsea rising from the water on a little promontory above a busy harbour. Now you look across grazing land to a sleepy village on a hill where only the ruined gateways ❷,❸ indicate how big the built-up area once was. The countryside around has an eerie, unsettled feeling as if the sea has not quite gone. Its contours preserve such a strong memory of the old coast that it is all too easy to imagine the tide raging back across the levels.

The sea's retreat was an episode in a long, uneasy relationship between town and shifting shore. Winchelsea is a new town in the sense of a settlement built from scratch according to a plan. The surprise is that it is more than 700 years old and the grid of wide streets that look like a 19th or 20th century development are based on a plan drawn up in 1288. Edward I founded the town to replace Old Winchelsea, a port located on a shingle spit somewhere in Rye Bay. It had been destroyed by a series of storms that battered the coast between 1233 and 1288, breaching the shingle bar and changing the topography of Rye Bay.

Old Winchelsea and Rye were members of the Confederation of the Cinque Ports, the alliance of coastal towns that provided the king with ships in return for special privileges. They were not among the original five and were given the status of 'Ancient Towns', after which the group became known as 'the Cinque Ports and the two Ancient Towns'. New Winchelsea inherited Old Winchelsea's role, and over the next 100 years endured destructive

INFORMATION

DISTANCE: 8.5 miles (options of 7 miles and 10 miles for Rye Circular).
TIME: 5 hours (3.5 and 5.5 hours for options).
MAP: OS Landranger 189 (Ashford & Romney Marsh); OS Explorer 125 (Romney Marsh) and 124 (Hastings and Bexhill).
START POINT: Winchelsea Station.
END POINT: Rye Station.
PUBLIC TRANSPORT: High-speed trains (with a surcharge) from St Pancras International, change at Ashford International. Slower trains (without surcharge) from other London stations. At the time of writing, trains from Ashford International to Rye are hourly but there is only one train every two hours to Winchelsea.
SWIMMING: In the sea at Winchelsea Beach.
PLACES OF INTEREST: Winchelsea town and St Thomas's church; Rye Harbour nature reserve; Camber Castle, Rye.
REFRESHMENTS: The New Inn, Winchelsea town (TN36 4FN, tel 01797 226252); Beach Café (TN36 4NG, tel 01797 223344) and Ship Inn (TN36 4LH, tel 01797 226767), Winchelsea Beach; various pubs and restaurants in Rye and a handy Budgens next door to Rye station.
WEEKEND SUGGESTION: Stay in Rye and next day take the train one stop to Three Oaks to do walk 25, Three Oaks to Hastings. Alternatively, just explore Rye one day and do the walk the next.

attacks by first French and then Castilian forces, but also enjoyed the benefits of commercial and military importance. All this came to an end when the harbour silted up in the late 15th century, precipitating a prolonged decline.

In the 18th century a calico industry helped support what remained of a population and during the Napoleonic Wars the town hosted a garrison once again, but by the late 19th century it had shrunk to a picturesque village celebrated by the discerning bourgeois from bigger towns as a delightful place to visit or settle. Famous residents included actress Ellen Terry, writer Ford Madox Ford and spymaster Vera Atkins. John Everett Millais painted The Blind Girl and The Random Shot there. Spike Milligan is buried in the churchyard. There were once several churches and the remaining one, St Thomas's ❷, stands in a spacious square amid gothic ruins. The interior seems disproportionately vast for the present town and yet even this is a remnant, as the nave occupies what was once just the transept of the massive 13th century church. Histories of town and church are on sale in the church and there is a small museum in Court Hall on the corner of High Street, opposite St Thomas's.

From Winchelsea the walk goes along the top of the former peninsula ❸ with views to the sea across Pett Level, an area of marsh and meadow criss-crossed by ditches and so flat that it mimics the sea, which once covered it. The Level is separated from the hillside by a particularly wide, deep ditch, the Royal Military Canal ❺. It runs through Rye and right round the back of Romney Marshes and was constructed during the Napoleonic Wars as part of coastal defences. Our walk drops down to follow the canal through reedy areas rich in bird life before crossing the Level to the shore, which

is bounded by a great dyke built in case one day the sea might try to return.

There is good swimming here at mid to high tide from a steeply sloping shingle beach, but as the sea recedes, sand and mud flats are gradually exposed until, by low tide, there is a long walk to the water and then a very long paddle until it is deep enough to swim. The bay is slightly sheltered and the shallows break the force of a big swell, so that the sea in summer is rarely too rough for swimming, but is often choppy enough to churn up the sand and mud to make the water look rather murky near the shore. As you swim out it clears pleasantly.

The settlement of Winchelsea Beach ❼-❽ is a largely 20th century development, which features a big caravan park and bungalows straggling along unpaved roads, screened by windswept hedges. Nearby is a large lake, Long Pit, the result of past shingle extraction and now part of Rye Harbour nature reserve, home to a variety of waterfowl and marshland birds.

The walk passes near Camber Castle ❾, an impressive ruin standing isolated on the marshes and, like Winchelsea town, stranded by the sea's retreat. It was built on a shingle spit to defend the large anchorage between Winchelsea and Rye. A tower of 1512 was later incorporated into a large military fort constructed on the order of Henry VIII between 1539 and 1544. The silting of the port made it obsolete by 1637 and Charles I ordered its demolition, but fortunately the order was not carried out. The interior is open to the public for brief periods during the summer (check details with English Heritage).

The destination, Rye, is a small town with a long history, many famous former residents and too much to see in a day, let alone in an hour or two after a long walk.

❶ WINCHELSEA

Leave Winchelsea station, turn right to cross the railway track onto a minor tarmac road leading towards the promontory on which Winchelsea stands. After about a quarter of a mile, cross the River Brede, walk through a small group of houses to a junction with the U-bend of the main A 259 and take a footpath to the right over a stile signed '1066 Country Walk', a newly developed walk which partially coincides with our route. The path passes a sewage works on your left, is briefly hedged on both sides, but soon goes over a stile into an open field, where it veers slightly left with a ditch and wood on the left. Pass two signed but faint paths off to the right and continue as the path starts to wind uphill and becomes a sunken track. Near the top follow the path left through a gate and past a beacon on a knoll to the right.

1 mile

❷ THE ANCIENT TOWN

After the beacon, as houses appear, head roughly straight on towards a long, low wooden building in front of a tiled house. Go through a gate to the right of the low building and follow a surfaced lane towards the main A259, where, looking left, you can see one of Winchelsea's medieval gates, the Pipewell Gate. Cross the main road to continue along Mill Road and take the first turning right, Hiham Green, to pass Court Hall and the town museum on the left. Cross a side road, High Street, to pass St Thomas's church on the

left and the New Inn on the right. Continue to the edge of town passing public lavatories on the left. The road bends right and passes a remnant of masonry on the left. Just to the right of this, go over a waymarked stile. (You have missed the stile if you reach a junction with the main A259.)

1.5 miles

❸ TO WICKHAM MANOR

From the stile follow a faint path across a field to an intersection with a fenced path, which you cross by means of two stiles to continue roughly straight on. The path, still quite faint, leads slightly downhill towards a large tree and a gap between trees. In the distance, ahead and to your left, you may see the ruins of one of the other town gateways, New Gate. Head for the gap in the trees, go through a gate with a waymarked sign and veer slightly right up a slope to where you get a good view of New Gate to the left and now behind you. Looking ahead there is a stone house, Wickham Manor, and to the left of it a rather beautiful barn. Go over a stile to the left of the barn to cross the Manor drive by means of another stile opposite.

2 miles

❹ THE SHORTCUT

Turn left on the Manor drive instead of crossing it, left again where it joins a road and then right onto a footpath heading down to the marshes to rejoin the main route at the bridge over the canal.

❹ THE MAIN WALK

After crossing the drive, cross the next field to the far left-hand corner. (Do not be misled by an old track to a gate on the left.) At the corner go over a waymarked stile and cross a tarmac lane into a field. Here the path marked on the map is straight on but, when we did the walk, it had been rerouted round the field edge to the right. So, follow it round, first parallel to the road, then turning left and then right through a gateway. Ignore a permissive path signed to the left and continue along a field edge with trees on your right to a strip of woodland serving as a wide hedgerow. Cross two stiles and continue through the next field (planted with sunflowers and wild flax when we walked). On the far side go over a stile by a lane, turn sharp left to go through a little gate beside a big gate onto a stony track. A few paces down turn right off the track on a waymarked but faint path. Look for two buildings ahead and keep them slightly to your left as you cross the field looking for a waymarked stile on the far side. The stile appears to lead into someone's grounds past a small building, but follow the path left of the building, then sharp left to skirt a house on the right and continue between overgrown hedges to a T-junction with a grassy track. Turn right downhill, enjoying great views over the marshes.

3 miles

❺ THE ROYAL MILITARY CANAL

At the bottom the path winds through a reed bed. Where it joins a track turn right and after a few paces turn left over a gated bridge crossing a drainage ditch. After the bridge turn left along the ditch. After about quarter of a mile, cross a small ditch joining the one on your left. Ignore a signed path to the left and continue to cross another much larger waterway, the Royal Military Canal. On the other side, at a T-junction, turn left and walk with the canal on your left for between quarter and half a mile to a waymarked cross-path where you turn right towards the sea. (The path on the left is the shortcut from Wickham Manor.)
3.75 miles

❻ ACROSS THE MARSHES

The path to the sea is not easy to follow despite waymarks on most of the gates. Start in the direction indicated by the signpost, keeping a small ditch on your right. This ditch ends just as it is nearly joined at right angles by a ditch on the left, but a gap between the ditches allows you to continue roughly straight on. Some way off to the right there should be a larger ditch running towards the sea, and the route lies roughly parallel to this but at varying distances. So, keep looking for the next gate and waymark while heading for the coast, bounded here by a road and dyke. The path joins the road at a rather inconspicuous signpost near the parallel ditch and a good field's distance to the right of a group of farm buildings.
4.5 miles

❼ THE BEACH

Cross the road, take steps to the top of the dyke and turn left to walk with the sea on your right. You can swim here, but there are groynes running parallel to the shore which, when partly under water, are a hazard. A little further on by Winchelsea Beach Café the road turns inland away from the shoreline and the swimming gets better because the groynes are at right angles to the shore. Continue along the shore, on the dyke or parallel path passing a caravan park. After about quarter of a mile pass some flats and a road and track both at right angles to the shore.
5.5 miles

❽ PAST LONG PIT

About 150 metres further on along the beach, turn onto a track heading slightly inland at an oblique angle. After a few metres, pass a track on the left and then two footpaths on the right, but continue to the end of the track where on the left there is a signed path, and a few paces further on an unsigned track. Take either as they meet after about quarter of a mile. The track is more pleasant as it runs beside a large lake known as Long Pit. Once past the lake the track runs through bushes, emerges to more open ground and reaches a junction with a cross-path. Turn right here along a path with messy hedges both sides. Go over a stile and continue on an almost invisible path across a field with a fence on the right, ignoring a farm track on the left. At the end of the field go through a gate and turn left on a track towards buildings, but just before the buildings take a path across open ground on the right towards Camber Castle.
6.5 miles

⑨ FROM CAMBER CASTLE

Before reaching the castle you will see two metal gates ahead, more or less side by side, both with a waymark sign. You can take either route, both to the left of the castle, but the quickest is the one more to the right and just to the right of a wire fence. (If you deviate to take a closer look at the castle, return to this path along the wire. Be careful because beyond the castle, slightly to the right, are new waymarked paths, not marked on the map we were using, which look as if they lead to Rye but are for exploring the nature reserve.) So, taking the path by the wire, continue across fields with a distant view of Rye church tower above the marshes. The path seems to head too far left, leading towards outlying houses strung along the A259. As you draw near, the path rises onto a low embankment that veers slightly right as it joins a larger embankment. This forms one edge of the Royal Military Canal, which separates you from the road and the houses.

7.5 miles

⑩ INTO RYE

Walk along the embankment towards Rye. After a metal gate follow the embankment and path as they veer away from the canal then curve back, heading to another metal gate. Go through this onto a narrow tarmac lane and walk on towards Rye. At Rye Harbour Road, where you see the masts of yachts along the river, turn left and cross the Military Canal to a junction with the busy A259, called at this point Winchelsea Road. Turn right to walk with the river on your right, passing tall black buildings on the far bank. Follow the road as it bends right to cross the river, and just after the bridge cross the A259 on a zebra crossing. At a small roundabout where the A259 turns right along the river's left bank, leave it to take Cinque Ports Street straight ahead. Ignore turnings right and left until you come to a V-junction where you take the left fork, and a little way along you will see a sign to the station to your right.

8.5 miles

Route option
Rye Circular (10 miles): To start the walk from Rye, turn right out of Rye station, leaving Budgens on your left, and turn left on a moderately main road. At the next junction turn right down Cinque Port Street to join the main A259, which you follow across the river and part way round a bend to the left. Near this take a track on the right, which leads to a waymarked footpath. Follow the path across flat pastureland, crossing a series of ditches, to join the Winchelsea to Rye route near the bridge over the River Brede, and pick up directions from step 1.

Margaret Dickinson, Bambi Ballard.

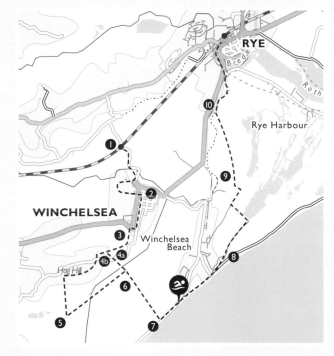

Walk 25

THREE OAKS TO HASTINGS, EAST SUSSEX

A short but hilly walk through pretty countryside with some scrambling to a lovely undeveloped stretch of shore, which is a naturist haven.

INFORMATION

DISTANCE: 6.5 miles.
TIME: 4 hours.
MAP: OS Landranger 199 (Eastbourne & Hastings); OS Explorer 124 (Hastings & Bexhill)
START POINT: Three Oaks Station.
END POINT: Hastings Station.
PUBLIC TRANSPORT: Train from Charing Cross or Victoria, or St Pancras International (faster but more expensive); change at Ashford International or Hastings onto a local service running between Ashford and Brighton via Hastings. At the time of writing this was an hourly service but only every other train stops at Three Oaks. NB Whichever route you take, you must be in the first carriage to get off at Three Oaks.
SWIMMING: In the sea at Covehurst Bay and Hastings.
PLACES OF INTEREST: Hastings Country Park and nature reserve; Hastings old town and resort.
REFRESHMENTS: The Three Oaks Inn (TN35 4NH, tel 01424 813303), Three Oaks; The White Hart Beefeater (TN35 4LW, tel 01424 813187), Guestling. Hastings has plenty of pubs, cafés and restaurants.
WEEKEND SUGGESTION: Combine with Walk 24, Winchelsea to Rye (see for details).

This beautiful walk wanders through gentle rolling fields and woodlands to reach one of the very few undeveloped stretches of coastline in the South East. The area is now a nature reserve rich in different habitats, including traditional meadowland and the tangled woodland of the undercliff. After reaching the sea the route follows the coastal path where there are challenging ups and downs, which make this a tougher walk than its distance would suggest.

The first swim on Fairlight Glen beach at Covehurst Bay **7** is at the bottom of a steep footpath where regular users have built a series of steps. It has no car access and no facilities and is recognised as a naturist beach. The rock here is crumbly yellow sandstone and mudstone, and frequent landslides have given rise to a shoreline of broken cliff and steep, wooded undercliffs, quite unlike the sheer chalk cliffs at Dover or Eastbourne. The track to the beach is sometimes obliterated by landfalls and when we did the walk it was officially closed, with notices telling you not to go down. These were, however, clearly ignored by many people and the path had been partially restored with rough wooden steps in the worst parts. It was passable but a scramble, not advisable for anyone unsure on their feet. Once down, you reach a rocky foreshore and beach that has stretches of sand at low tide, but is reduced to a narrow, rocky strip at high tide.

According to some naturist websites, Fairlight Glen was the first beach to be recognised by a local council as officially naturist, in 1978. This sounds very late but the key may be the term 'officially', since long before the 1970s some beaches were accepted by custom and practice as nudist areas. Apparently the 'official' designation

was withdrawn from Fairlight in 1999, but that probably made little difference to those who use the beach, whether drawn by the freedom to be naked or by its peaceful seclusion, free from roads, cars and buildings.

Naturism as a movement dates back over a century. It was in Germany that the first real nudist club, Freilichpark, opened in 1903. In England the first organised manifestation was the English Gymnosophical Society formed in 1922, in a very loose sense a forerunner of British Naturism, the present-day federation of naturist societies.

Germany, however, was not the absolute pioneer. Surprisingly, it turns out that the first known naturist association in the world was in India, although presumably British by culture. It was the Fellowship for the Naked Trust founded in 1891 by Charles Edward Gordon Crawford, a District and Sessions Judge for the Bombay Civil Service, and it appears to have attracted only two other members, the sons of a British missionary. Perhaps there is a bizarre justice in India laying claim to this 'first' given that its dominant public culture today is intensely prudish. Naturism, as an organised movement, rather than simply liking to go naked now and again, only makes sense as a reaction to prudery, and even catches from the prudish a faint echo of coercion. Happily, there is none of this in Fairlight Glen, where no one will tick you off if you choose to wear a costume.

The second opportunity to swim is at the end of the walk, off Hastings beach **❾**, which is also a mixture of shingle and sand, a town beach but rarely crowded. Hastings itself is an interesting place with a long maritime history and a dramatic, hilly site overlooked by the ruined castle. It is one of the Cinque Ports, once had a major fishing industry and still has the largest beach-based fishing fleet in England. There are remnants of the elegant resort it became in the 18th and 19th centuries, but sadly it has declined more than many of the old resorts, and a lot of the pretty houses look badly in need of repainting.

DIRECTIONS

❶ FROM THREE OAKS

Turn left out of the station on a road that crosses the railway line. Just on the other side of the line turn left into a very minor road, Eight Acre Lane, which runs parallel to the railway line and, after about quarter of a mile, goes under it to continue parallel to it on the other side. Ignore a footpath on the left as you go under the railway and another one a little further on, which you may miss as it is not well marked. Take the next FP on the left, shortly after passing a road to the right, Rock Lane, and just after passing buildings on the right and left sides of the lane. The FP is what looks like the second of four driveways. There is a sign but it is not easy to spot.

I mile

❷ CROSSING THE A259

Take the path through a wood following signs, which distinguish it from a private track. After about 300 metres you reach a clearing. Veer uphill, to the right, looking out for a faintly marked path crossing the grass to a signpost on the other side of the clearing. At the sign-post there is a good view back over the fields.

DIRECTIONS

The path continues through the wood to bring you out on a big main road, the A259.
1.5 miles

❸ HASTINGS COUNTRY PARK

Turn right and walk a little way along the road round a slight bend, and look for a poorly marked path on the other side which will lead you on in the direction you were taking before you met the road. Cross the road with care, go over the stile and follow the path through a field, keeping along the fence on the left-hand edge. At the signpost marked Hastings Country Park continue to the left of some houses to reach a minor road. Cross this and continue on a narrow path that very soon turns sharp right through

what appears to be a private driveway, but which is indicated by a FP sign. Pass some houses and a small field/garden to find a narrow path straight on and slightly downhill.

❹ The next bit is tricky. The path goes through a field and past some trees into another field where one path goes straight on, but you turn right down a rather faint path. If you turn too early, you will come across a small, private stone circle; retrace your steps and continue straight on. If you pass the turning, you come to a hard track, actually the drive to someone's house, and this indicates you have missed the turning. Go back. The correct turning heads down to the corner

of the field, into a steep dip, over a little bridge and up the other side through some woods.
2 miles

❺ FAIRLIGHT LODGE HOTEL

Walk through a field, which when we did the walk had been cleared along the path. Continue uphill, with the hedge line to your right. You will soon see a large hall, with turrets on your left, which is the hotel. At the top of the hill follow a path on the left, cut through the crops, and into the woods above the hotel. Follow the wooden fence, and continue past the large, three-truncked, boundary beech tree. Cross a gravel driveway and continue along the path over a stile. Follow this path until you reach a minor road, Fairlight Road.
3 miles

❻ TO FAIRLIGHT GLEN

Cross the road and look for a continuation of your path to the right, running parallel with the road, until you reach a left turn towards the coast. After about 200 metres, ignore a path crossing at right angles and continue downhill on steps by the side of a wood until, after another quarter of a mile, you reach the main cliff top path. You will begin to see signs for Fairlight Glen beach.
3.5 miles

❼ DOWN TO THE SEA

Turn right along the cliff top path, initially up a series of steps, until you reach a turning to the left near a stream, which will take you down to the beach. As mentioned in the description of the swim, this was

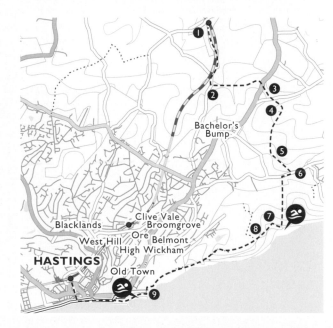

fenced off with a warning sign when we did the walk, but was evidently regularly used. From this point it is rather a steep scramble down to the beach, which would probably be slippery when wet. After your swim go back up the track and turn right at the cliff top path to walk on in a westerly direction.
4 miles

❽ ON THE CLIFF TOPS
From here follow a clearly marked cliff top path up and down until you reach the top of the funicular railway above Hastings. On our walk, several paths closest to the coast had been temporarily closed due to weather damage. For an alternative and less hilly route further inland, follow the signs for Barley Lane car park, turn left out of the car park and follow the road past the caravan park. When you come to a cliff-top field, cross it diagonally to the left until you reach the top of the funicular.
5.5 miles

❾ HASTINGS
Go down the steps by the funicular and continue into the old town until you reach the sea front. Walk to the west along the front until, about halfway to the pier, you should see a sign to the station some way after a roundabout and at the second of two T-junctions. Head inland following signs or taking Harold Place and its continuation, Havelock Road, to reach the station, about a quarter of a mile away from the front.
6.5 miles

Margaret Dickinson, Emma Beatrice Clark.

Walk 26

BERWICK TO SEAFORD, EAST SUSSEX

The walk is through classic downland and over high cliffs, with spectacular views of the Seven Sisters and a fantastic swim in the sea at Cuckmere Haven.

INFORMATION

DISTANCE: 9.5 miles.
TIME: 5 hours.
MAP: OS Landranger 199 (Eastbourne & Hastings); OS Explorer 123 (Eastbourne & Beachy Head).
START POINT: Berwick Station.
END POINT: Seaford Station.
PUBLIC TRANSPORT: From London Victoria take the Eastbourne train and change at Lewes or Polegate. The train may be signalled to Ore and Littlehampton, in which case it will divide, usually at Haywards Heath; make sure to travel in the right section. Return from Seaford, usually with a change at Lewes.
SWIMMING: In the sea at Cuckmere Haven or Seaford; in the Cuckmere River at high tide.
PLACES OF INTEREST: Berwick church; Alfriston old village; West Dean; views of Seven Sisters.
REFRESHMENTS: Cricketers' Arms (BN26 6SP, tel 01323 870469), Berwick; Alfriston has many pubs and restaurants; The Cuckmere Inn (BN25 4AB, tel 01323 892 247), Seaford.
WEEKEND SUGGESTIONS: After the walk, stay in Seaford where there are hotels and B&Bs, or take the train to Southease and stay in the South Downs Youth Hostel (BN8 6JS, tel 0845 371 9574). The next day do Walk 27, Southease to Newhaven. Alternatively, do the walk in two parts, leaving time to enjoy the sights and sample pubs and cafés. You can stay in Alfriston where accommodation includes the Frog Firle Youth Hostel (BN26 5TT, tel 0845 371 9101).

This walk is a superb introduction to the South Downs. It takes in Berwick village with its wonderful painted church ❶, then heads across fields, down through Alfriston ❷, over the river and along the valley, below the edge of the Downs, then through woods, eventually arriving at the sea at Cuckmere Haven. After swimming, you can follow the cliff path west to Seaford, with brilliant views of the Seven Sisters chalk cliffs behind.

As well as striking landscapes and great swimming, there is art and history to enjoy. Berwick church is famous for a series of 20th century murals, painted during the Second World War by the Bloomsbury artists Duncan Grant, Vanessa Bell and Quentin Bell. Biblical scenes feature local people and are depicted as taking place in the surrounding area, which the artists knew well. Duncan Grant and Vanessa Bell's house, Charleston Farmhouse (not to be confused with Charleston Manor), is walking distance away, while Monk's House, belonging to Vanessa's sister Virginia Woolf and her husband Leonard, is in the village of Rodmell, just a little further west. The area has long been popular with artists and writers, and its chalk hills feature prominently in paintings by Paul Nash and Eric Ravilious. The famous hymn 'Morning has broken' was written in Alfriston by Eleanor Farjeon in 1931 and was inspired by the East Sussex countryside.

Alfriston is a big village, almost a small town, which has become a busy tourist destination. It is especially known for the 14th century timber-frame Clergy House, the first building taken on by the National Trust. It also has a grand parish church and streets of attractive old houses. Between the 14th and 16th centuries it

was a popular resting place for monks making their pilgrimage across East Sussex from Battle Abbey to Chichester Cathedral to visit the shrine of St Richard. Like many coastal settlements it was involved in smuggling, but industry also developed, principally a tannery and glove factory, in the late 18th and early 19th centuries when troops were settled there during the Napoleonic Wars.

The first opportunity to swim in the sea is on the west side of Cuckmere Haven ❻ from a sloping shingle beach where the sea is usually clear and the views are lovely. If the sea is rough, an alternative is to swim at very high tide in the Cuckmere River, a little upstream from its mouth. Be aware of the tidal current though, which may be too strong to swim against. There is another chance to swim from Seaford beach ❼, which is gravelly shingle, backed by uninspired seaside development, but offers good swimming.

DIRECTIONS

❶ BERWICK
Come out of the station onto a narrow but sometimes busy road. Turn right (if you arrived on an eastbound train, you cross the railway line) and almost immediately take a bridleway on the right next to a corrugated iron building and across the road from the Berwick Inn. Follow it across fields for less than half a mile to Stonery Farm, which is not signed but where there is a gate with the Vanguard Way (VGW) sign indicating left. Follow the sign on a tarmac track for a short distance to a minor road. Cross the road, take a few paces left and continue on the VGW almost straight on, but slightly diagonally left through fields. After a stile beside a metal gate the path turns right to follow the hedge on the right to the corner of the field and then on to the busy A27. Cross with care and turn left to take a small, signed lane to the right towards Berwick village.
1.5 miles

❷ ALFRISTON
From Berwick churchyard leave by a little gate, ignore a path ahead and turn right on the VGW, which leads in roughly the direction you have been travelling. After about half a mile the path joins a lane, then crosses another to continue into Alfriston. More or less opposite where you meet the main road through Alfriston, just after the village cross, take a narrow track leading to the river. If you miss it and come to the church, then turn left off the road and pass the church on your right to reach the riverside path and a small white footbridge. (Here, instead of following steps 3 and 4 you could remain on the right bank and follow the river path to rejoin the route at Exceat Bridge, step 5.)
2.5 miles

❸ THE CUCKMERE VALLEY
Cross the footbridge. Continue to a road and turn right on a path beside it, which then cuts across a field and joins the road again just before Litlington.
3.5 miles

❹ LITLINGTON TO WEST DEAN
Walk through Litlington and at the end of the village take a track left for a short distance and then take a FP, part of the South Downs Way, branching

right and heading south, roughly parallel to and above the road. Follow the South Downs Way past Charleston Manor, through a wood and into West Dean. Here the route is complicated because there are many small lanes and paths. As you enter the hamlet, walk to the bottom of the road and turn right alongside the river and follow a FP heading straight into a wood. Almost at once take another path to the right and follow it as it turns to the left and then left again, running parallel to the edge of the wood. It will lead you out onto the A259.

5.5 miles

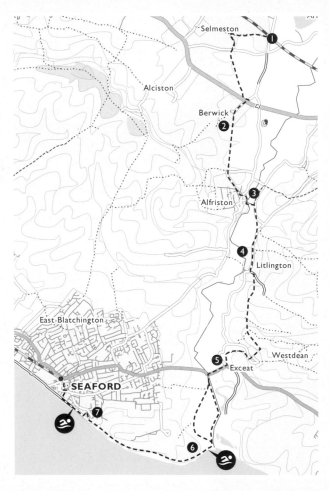

(Here you could decide to cut the walk short, as there is a regular bus service to Eastbourne or Brighton. In that case, to swim, cross the road and walk straight on along a track to the main beach on the left bank of the river.)

⑤ EXCEAT BRIDGE

To continue on our route, do not take this track to the beach. Instead, turn right and walk for about 200 metres along the main road to cross the Cuckmere River on the Exceat Bridge. Just after the bridge, by the Cuckmere Inn, take a path on the left, which leads down to the beach on the right (west) bank of the river. A few yards down, the path divides and you can either take the left path along the river or the right branch, the VGW, along the edge of the flood plain. They both lead to the beach at Cuckmere Haven.

7 miles

⑥ CUCKMERE HAVEN

After your sea swim follow the cliff path westwards. It is a steep climb and you have great views back to the Seven Sisters. The path leads you past Seaford Head nature reserve and into the outskirts of Seaford, turning a little inland as you approach the town.

8.5 miles

⑦ SEAFORD

Walk along the front, turn right at The Causeway, pass the Wellington pub, cross Steyn Road and turn left on Church Street to the station.

9.5 miles

Margaret Dickinson, Melanie Reed

Walk 27

SOUTHEASE TO NEWHAVEN, EAST SUSSEX

This walk begins with panoramic views from Itford Hill on the South Downs Way, then leads to the sea and edge-lands that border industrial Newhaven.

INFORMATION

DISTANCE: 10 miles.
TIME: 5 hours.
MAP: OS Landranger 198 (Brighton & Lewes); OS Explorer 123 (Eastbourne & Beachy Head). The hamlet of Southease is on Explorer 122, not 123, but is easy to find without the second map.
START POINT: Southease Station.
END POINT: Newhaven Harbour Station.
PUBLIC TRANSPORT: Train from London Victoria to Southease, change at Lewes. Return from Newhaven Harbour, change at Lewes. Buy a day return to Newhaven Harbour.
SWIMMING: In the sea between Bishopstone and Tide Mills.
PLACES OF INTEREST: Southease church; Tide Mills ruined village and tide mill.
REFRESHMENTS: The only cafés on the route are the Courtyard Café at South Downs YHA (BN8 6JS tel 0845 371 9574), Southease, and the Shorebreak Café at the Newhaven and Seaford sailing club (BN25 2QR tel 01323 890077), Seaford.
WEEKEND SUGGESTION: Combine the walk with Walk 26, Berwick to Seaford (see for details).

*T*his is a walk of contrasts, between tranquil Southease with its round-towered church, the sweeping contours of Itford Hill and the South Downs, and the industrial present and remains of Newhaven. It was also, for us, a walk of contrasting weather. We were struck by how quiet the South Downs Way was on a sunny Spring Bank Holiday Saturday morning. Perhaps other walkers had not ignored the weather forecast: the hail and rain, when it came, threw us off course and laughed at our waterproofs.

Southease train station is a lovely starting point, entirely surrounded by fields that were full of buttercups in late May, almost as far as the eye could see. It feels a world away from London, with a hand-operated level crossing for use by authorised vehicles only. A short detour to the hamlet of Southease is well worth taking. The Domesday Book describes a thriving community at Southease in 1068: at that time 46 villagers supplied 38,500 herring to the abbot of St Peter's in Winchester, some 90 miles away. Southease now has about 50 inhabitants, and while it has no shop or pub, it does, according to a booklet we picked up in the church, have its very own Church Cleaners' Union.

A tiny lane takes you to the (no longer swinging) Swing Bridge over the River Ouse and alongside a stream and hedgerow with wild roses. We heard whitethroats, chiffchaffs and song thrushes as we walked. The Norman church, with its round flint tower, has the remains of 13th century coloured New Testament frescos, uncovered in the 1930s. A modern stained glass window in the west wall works rather well with the wall paintings. You can fill a water bottle from a tap outside the church, in preparation for the climb up Itford Hill.

Crossing back through the station, you approach Itford Hill by going round the flint outbuildings of Itford Farm, imaginatively converted into the South Downs Youth Hostel. Look out for the exhibition of photographs and oral history of the farm (and the lovely café). Soon, as you climb, you begin to see the Sussex countryside pan out below you. After an initial steep section you are rewarded with a view of one of the wonderful sweeping curves that characterise the Downs, and a slightly gentler incline. The further you climb, the more you can see of the River Ouse, flowing from what you begin to realise is Lewes to the north, down to Newhaven in the south. Southease church comes into view, but soon becomes just a tiny dot on a huge landscape.

A vast patchwork of agriculture and villages opens up to the north once you are on Itford Hill ❸, and as you continue up the South Downs Way ridge you see, to the south, ever more of the sea beyond – and the chimneys and distant gleaming roofs of Newhaven's huge new incinerator. But it is far away and is intriguing, rather than troubling. There are trees up here, bravely hugging the hillside, their shapes sculpted by the wind. Listen out for skylarks, too. Before the radio station at the top you begin your descent, down to the right towards the sea.

The valleys here are called bottoms. There is a Breaky Bottom, a Cow Wish Bottom and even a Loose Bottom. You head through rolling hillsides towards Poverty Bottom, a tiny sunken lane with high hedgerows on either side. At the little hamlet of Norton ❺ you take what turns out to be an exhilarating path up to a ridge that overlooks the sea, the village of Bishopstone and its pretty church and, in the distance, the first two of the Seven Sisters – the white cliffs that tower over the sea beyond Seaford, with Cuckmere Haven between them.

Once you descend the ridge it is not far to the sea. We were told that the best place to access fairly deep water at any tide is outside the Newhaven and Seaford Sailing Club, near where you first reach the sea front. On our stormy May walk it was too rough to swim, but on a sunny July day we enjoyed two long swims in calm turquoise water off the long shingle beach, one by the sailing club and the other near Tide Mills ❾. Behind the beach used to stand a tide mill, built in 1761 to mill grain, and operated by tidal power. Some 100 workers, housed in nearby cottages, worked five pairs of millstones to produce up to 1,200 sacks of flour each week. You can still see the remains of the buildings.

Our inclination was to walk along the sea front rather than turning inland at Tide Mills, but we then found ourselves the wrong side of Mill Creek and had to take a rather grim path along high security fences to reach the station. Better to follow the Vanguard Way, which runs north of the Creek. Reaching Newhaven Harbour station at the weekend, it is hard to believe that trains will arrive or stop there, but rest assured they do!

❶ SOUTHEASE

From Southease station cross the railway bridge and pick up the lane that winds first alongside the railway tracks and then turns right to cross the River Ouse. After half a mile the lane goes gently uphill to Southease and the church. After visiting the church, retrace your steps to the station.
1 mile

❷ ITFORD HILL

Cross back over the railway bridge and follow the lane and South Downs Way signposts eastwards to Itford Hill. Wind round to the right of Itford Farm, now South Downs YHA, and the Courtyard Café, and cross the bridge over the A26, to begin the climb up Itford Hill. The track first curves right, in parallel with the road below, and then sweeps more gently up to the left and turns into a grassy path. Near a short post with a waymark, it sweeps further left to a fence where a bridleway sign indicates the track runs along the left of the fence. The track then swings to the right to reach the top of Itford Hill, marked by a trig point.
2.5 miles

❸ OFF THE SOUTH DOWNS WAY

Continue more gently uphill, on the ridge of the South Downs Way, through a gate towards the radio station masts. Before you reach the radio station, after a second gate and at a path crossing, turn right to leave the South Downs Way. A bridleway sign shows there is a right of way, but there is no visible path. Head for the gate on the other side of the field, after which a path becomes more obvious. Continue gently downhill, through a second gate towards the hill ahead.
4 miles

❹ OVER THE DOWNS

As you approach the hill, the path divides. Take the left fork, with a slope falling away steeply to your left, to go up then down the hill. Almost a mile after the fork you come to a confusing junction of paths. Clear tracks lead to the right and straight ahead, downhill. There appears to be a path to the left, though there is none marked on the map. Ignore these and take the tiny and unmarked bridleway that goes through the field to your right, taking you slightly to the right of the wide downhill track.
5.5 miles

❺ TO POVERTY BOTTOM

Take the bridleway down through the field, keeping just left of the spur of the hill, to cross a path at a dip at the end of the field. Continue straight on downhill into Poverty Bottom, a lovely path with high hedges on both sides. This becomes a wide track then a tarmac road, where you pass some old buildings, apparently used for some high-security purpose. You reach the hamlet of Norton, with one lane leading ahead and one turning left.
6.5 miles

6 ABOVE BISHOPSTONE

Instead of taking either lane, take the footpath to the right before a house named Pond End, and go past the pond (which sometimes dries up). Climb a fairly steep hill to a ridge, which sweeps round to the left. Do not take the path that crosses the ridge, which leads to Newhaven, but keep on the path that contours left, round with the ridge. Newhaven's urban sprawl is over to the west, with its breakwater reaching far into the sea: you can screen this by dropping slightly to the grassy path just below the crest of the ridge. Continue below the ridge, with a fence to your right and another to your left, which gradually converge at the first of two stiles; cross both.

7.5 miles

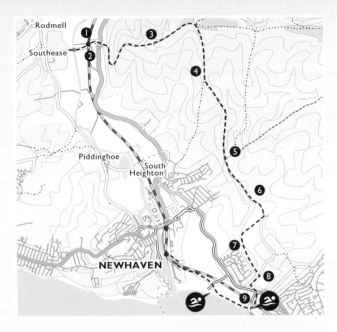

7 TOWARDS THE SEA

Follow a wide grassy track slightly upwards and then downhill. To keep on the right of way, cross a rather overgrown stile below a house on the right, a little over halfway down. Turn left and follow the path down between two fences to the bottom of the field. Turn right on a path through trees to a minor road, Bishopstone Road, and turn right along it. (If the stile is too overgrown it may be easier to stay on the grassy track and climb over the locked gate at the bottom.)

8 miles

8 TO THE SEA FRONT

With houses now on your right, walk towards the main A259 and take a little footpath left to cut off the corner. Cross the A259 and take the FP in front of you and to the left, aiming for the railway bridge. Take the road under the bridge and, as you approach the sea front, The Newhaven and Seaford Sailing Club and café will be on your right. This is a good place to swim.

8.5 miles

9 TIDE MILLS AND NEWHAVEN

Walk west past the sailing club and a caravan/campsite on your right towards a sign for Tide Mills. To the right of this is a signpost for the Vanguard Way. You can decide here to either take the Vanguard Way or walk nearer the beach on a concrete track with rails. If you choose the latter, turn right when you reach the ruined tide mill to cross the creek. Part way between the creek and the railway rejoin the Vanguard Way by turning left onto a signed FP by a ruined building. The path continues with the creek on the left and the railway on the right until it crosses the railway by a bridge. Turn left to reach the gates of the ferry port. Go through them and turn right to Newhaven Harbour station.

10 miles

Armorer Wason, Maggie Jennings.

ARUNDEL TO LITTLEHAMPTON, WEST SUSSEX

Starting with views of Arundel castle, this walk takes in ancient woodland, Norman churches, the River Arun and a sea swim at a marine nature reserve.

*A*rundel lies on the south side of the South Downs, where the River Arun has cut a clear way through the chalk hills, providing a natural route south. The town dates back to Roman times and by 1066 was a busy market and port. The famous castle has been ruined and rebuilt several times so the building you see today is mainly 19th century. Near the town bridge are ruins of a 13th century Dominican friary and the 14th century church of St Nicholas. The town website has a good historical section giving details about some of the old houses, including numbers 37-41 and 71 High Street. If you take Maltravers Street, look at number 8, the remains of a three-bayed hall house with a timber frame roof, and number 79 with a similar roof.

From the 16th century a series of navigational improvements made the river navigable beyond Arundel ❶ and increased the town's importance as a port. Eventually, in 1816 the Arun and Wey Junction Canal was opened, providing a navigable link via the Wey and the Thames all the way between London and the sea at Littlehampton, but the route was never as profitable as hoped and closed in 1871. By then the railways were eclipsing the waterways and Littlehampton took over as the port on the Arun.

After leaving Arundel the walk heads south towards the sea over fairly flat land with distant views of the Downs. Much of our route is beside the tidal River Arun, but at first the walk branches away over higher ground to pass through the remains of an ancient forest at Tortington Common ❷.

Two remarkable early churches are worth stopping for. St Mary Magdalene in Tortington ❷ is predominantly 12th century,

INFORMATION

DISTANCE: 10 miles.
TIME: 5.5 hours.
MAP: OS Landranger 197 (Chichester & the Downs); OS Explorer 121 (Arundel & Pulborough).
START POINT: Arundel Station.
END POINT: Littlehampton Station.
PUBLIC TRANSPORT: Train from London Victoria. Trains destination Littlehampton and Orr divide en route, so sit in correct section.
SWIMMING: In the sea between Atherington and Littlehampton West beach. Possible swims in the River Arun at very high tide.
PLACES OF INTEREST: Arundel town and castle; Tortington church, Ford church; Atherington shoreline; Littlehampton port and old resort.
REFRESHMENTS: Choices in Arundel and Littlehampton: West Beach Café (BN17 5DL tel 01903 718153), Littlehampton. Halfway along the route is Ship and Anchor (BN18 0BJ, tel 01243 551747), Ford.
WEEKEND SUGGESTIONS: Stay the first day in Arundel. There is much to see and a pleasant lido near Arundel Bridge. To enjoy the lovely Arun valley get off the train at Amberley and walk down the river by a signed path to Arundel. To spend more time on the coast, split the walk at Littlehampton and overnight there. Next day resume the route to West Beach and continue by the sea westwards five miles to Bognor Regis and the train home.

connected with the now ruined Tortington Priory, and is known for grotesque carved figures. Look for the carvings over the door and the 'beak heads' over the chancel arch – strange monsters with beaks, tongues and squid-like tentacles, which would originally have been brightly painted. In the north aisle there are two fine Kempe Studio stained glass windows from 1896. The second church, St Andrew-by-the-Ford ❸, is part Saxon, part Norman and has remains of medieval wall paintings. There are good leaflets giving more details on sale in both churches.

Confident, strong swimmers may consider swimming in the Arun near Tortington ❸. There is a famous annual event, the Ironman Swim between Ford Marina and Arundel, but that is a very different affair from a casual dip. Swimming in the river is only feasible at very high tide and even then conditions are daunting. The banks are reinforced with concrete, which is good for entry but makes getting out up a smooth and potentially slimy slope quite tricky. The tidal current is very strong, so that unless the tide is exactly on the turn swimmers may find it impossible to return to the spot where they entered. If everyone in your party wants to swim, make sure someone tests the ease of getting out unaided before all the others plunge in.

The walk reaches the sea to the west of Littlehampton where the shoreline is open, backed by areas of shingle, marsh and sand dune, which is a nature reserve ❺ ❻. The area seems to be popular with walkers but is rarely crowded. On one occasion, under a hot summer sun when the sea reflected back a blazing, blue sky, we were surprised to find the warm beach relatively empty. Another time, on a blustery November day when the waters were a shifting mixture of grey-browns, we were almost equally surprised to find that we did not have the windswept beach entirely to ourselves.

The sea swim is good between high and mid tide. There is a sloping, shingle beach with a nearly flat expanse of sand below it. At high tide you swim off the shingle slope, which may be tricky if the sea is rough. Around mid tide the sand makes for a more comfortable entry, but when the tide is lower still the water becomes too shallow and remains so for a very long way out. Our first time here we went in after mid tide, on the ebb, and swam out merrily in shallow water assuming that it would get deeper. It did not and meanwhile the tide dropped, stranding us ankle deep far from the shore. At that stage we found that for some time we had not been swimming over sand, but over sharp, slippery rocks that made the long paddle back painfully difficult. As the tide goes out still further the sea exposes an immense stretch of sand and rock, which has a certain bleak beauty and is fun for young children, but discouraging for would-be swimmers.

① THROUGH ARUNDEL

Follow the station slip road onto the main A27 to a roundabout. Take the second exit straight on towards Arundel and soon turn off right on a signed path to the river. Follow the path until it brings you back onto the road, Queen Street, just before Arundel Bridge. Cross to enter Arundel and enjoy views of the old town. Continue slightly left and straight on up the busy High Street and shortly turn left, taking either Tarrant Street or Maltravers Street, both of which lead to a big roundabout on the A27.

I mile

② TO TORTINGTON

Go left round the roundabout to cross the A27 and on the other side take a path to your right marked 'Underpass', but instead of bearing left under the road, go on to the river and turn right along the bank. Continue for a little over half a mile to take a signposted path to the right that

may be rather overgrown. On reaching Ford Road turn right then left up Maxwell Road, a side road with suburban houses. Pass a left turning, continuing straight along Torton Hill Road to turn left onto Dalloway Road at a T-junction. After a short distance, where the road turns towards the right, look for a signposted but hard-to-see footpath going roughly straight ahead into the woods. Continue on the path across two very minor roads and on through woods. After about half a mile, after a small bridge over a brook, take a FP to the left, which soon leads out of the woods, across fields, swerves left and reaches a minor road by some farm buildings. Turn right on the road. Soon pass on the left Tortington Manor, a small development that used to be a college, and where the road turns left enter the hamlet of Tortington, where you may want to stop and look at the church.

3.5 miles

③ TO FORD

Just after the hamlet, the minor road joins the busier Ford Road. Cross it and take a track straight on to rejoin the river path. Turn right, downstream. If you have arranged to be here at high tide this is a good place to swim as there are likely to be fishermen near the railway bridge downstream. Follow the river path to the railway bridge, the hamlet of Ford and the Ship and Anchor pub. Shortly after the railway bridge there is a small

creek from which a path goes off to Ford church, a small but worthwhile diversion.

5 miles

④ PAST CLIMPING

Retrace your steps from the church to the river path and continue downstream for nearly two miles, passing reed beds and stands of trees. After the first mile there are a few buildings away on the right on the edge of Climping, which include a prison. After the second mile, where you can hear and see the main A259 which skirts around Littlehampton, you come to a metal fence where you have to go close to the river to find a small gate.

7 miles

⑤ LITTLEHAMPTON MARINA

Continue on the riverside path under the A259 and through a small metal gate beside a larger metal gate into a car park. Go through the car park and continue to walk on a small road along the river, past Littlehampton Marina and a café/bar. This is an industrialised stretch of river with gasholders and factories on the far side and a container park on the near side. On reaching a road junction and footbridge over the Arun, ignore the bridge and follow Ferry Road briefly as it sweeps right, but turn off left to continue your previous direction on Rope Walk, a little road with a café on the left and chalets on the right. Soon there is a junction where a private driveway goes roughly straight on. To the right of it is a footpath, a driveway signed to West Beach car park, and another FP. Take this last FP on the right, which starts between fences and has a golf course on the left and a wood on the right. The path is enclosed by trees in places and passes by reedy areas. At a junction with another path bear left and soon afterwards emerge onto the beach by a stone platform supporting an information board. You will turn left to return to Littlehampton, but first enjoy a swim in the sea. **8.5 miles**

❻ LITTLEHAMPTON WEST BEACH

Walk eastwards along the beach until you reach the large wooden groyne marking the channel of the Arun. There is a car park here and the small West Beach Café. Turn inland and walk with the Arun on your right. Keep as close to the water as you can and look out for interesting jetties, boats and the decaying hulls of older boats. You have to walk part of the way on a driveway separated from the river by boatyards and sheds, but soon turn off onto a FP that takes you closer to the river again and returns you to the junction near the footbridge. Retrace your steps to the footbridge, now on your right. Cross the Arun, turn right on the road the other side and you will soon see the station. **10 miles**

Margaret Dickinson, Maggie Jennings

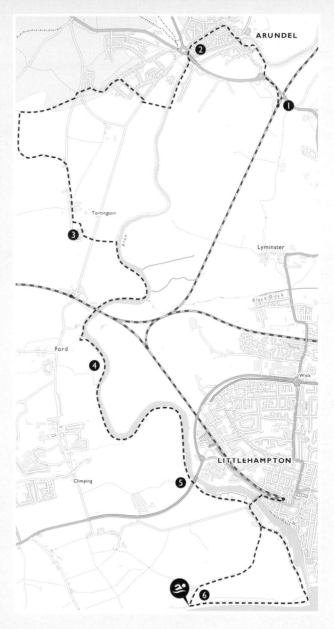

205

CONTRIBUTORS

BAMBI BALLARD
Bambi's career has spanned working for filmmaker Michael Cacoyannis in Greece, making costumes for bands and restoring silent films in Paris. She has been a keen walker since childhood, with her parents in Africa, Spain and Italy, on her own in Greece, London and Paris, and, after a long hiatus, with Margaret Dickinson in the countryside round London.

ROSALIND BAYLEY
Rosalind has enjoyed following trails and plunging into the unknown as both a historian and housing journalist. She wrote *To Paradise by Way of Gospel Oak*, an urban micro-history that celebrates a successful battle against gentrification in the 1970s.

ANGUS BOULTON
Angus is a photographer and filmmaker. As a Yorkshireman living in central London, participating in group walks through the Home Counties was initially undertaken as a form of photographic location research, but really is a sociable way to take some exercise. He has been known to swim, in the sea.

FRANCES CAIRNCROSS
Frances was head of Exeter College, Oxford, for ten years until the end of September 2014. She swam regularly in the Thames off Port Meadow. Now back in London, she is delighted to be back in the equally lovely Ladies' Pond.

MARY CANE
Mary learned to swim in the River Trent as a child from the family boat, Majessa. She started daily

swimming in Kenwood Ladies' Pond in 1982 to alleviate stress during her terms as a Labour councillor for Camden. She has run social enterprises and been a journalist and a campaigner. She helped fellow pond lover Ann Griswold edit *The Hungry Winter Swimmer* (KLPA 2002), a compilation of swimmers' recipes, poems and cartoons.

CATH CINNAMON
Cath is a retired English and media teacher, Buddhist, knitter and fanatical life-long swimmer.

EMMA BEATRICE CLARK
Emma is a designer/maker who has also written and illustrated two children's picture books. Having grown up in rural Bedfordshire, Kenwood Ladies' Pond and the surrounding Heath provide an essential connection with the natural world she explored avidly as a child and continues to love as an adult.

RUTH CORNEY
Ruth is an award-winning photographer. She has had several exhibitions and publications that bear testament to her passion for the Hampstead ponds and Parliament Hill Lido. She is also trying to be a year round pond swimmer!

SALLY DAVEY
Sally is the founder of Tripbod, a website that connects travellers with trusted locals in their destination to help uncover hidden gems (now part of TripAdvisor). Sally was born and raised in the Lake District so walking and water are in her soul, making the Kenwood ponds a vital part of her life in London.

MARGARET DICKINSON
Margaret is a filmmaker and writer who has loved country walking and swimming in ponds, rivers and the sea since childhood. She produced the film *City Swimmers* used in the 2004/5 campaign to save swimming on Hampstead Heath.

CLARISSA DORNER
After 35 years in Hampshire, Clarissa now lives in central London. The Ladies' Pond is a special place for her and the closest approximation to swimming in the Dorset River Stour where she grew up.

BRIONY FANE
Briony is a research psychologist with a passion for open water swimming and endurance sports.

LYNDA FRANKLIN
Lynda is an all-season pond, lido, river and sea swimmer. She is a secondary teacher in Islington and member of London Independent Photography.

JO GOLDSWORTHY
Jo is a former publisher, now an editorial consultant. A life-long hiker and walker, she became a wild swimming convert after moving to north London 30 years ago and discovering the joys of the Ladies' Pond, where she now swims through the year.

KATHREIN GÜNTHER
Kathrein is a German Londoner who has been going on walks with Margaret for some ten years now. The inspiring company, beautiful scenery, encounters with the local flora and fauna, and the occasional visits to wayside pubs have made her a devoted fan of walking. She works as a corporate film and video producer.

SHULA HAWES
Shula loves being outdoors, whether cycling, walking, stargazing or camping. Since discovering the Hampstead ponds 18 months ago, outdoor swimming has become an increasingly important part of her life. She is currently making a short film about the Kenwood Ladies'

Pond and the women who swim there. Her work is running creative projects in care homes.

MAGGIE JENNINGS
Missing her childhood in Devon, Maggie enjoys immersing herself in water and countryside in sun, rain or snow. She has greatly enjoyed walking and swimming for this book, and as an artist has taken the opportunity to make many sketches of the walks. Wild swimming could be viewed as her replacement stimulant now she has retired as a professional wrestler.

HANNAH PEARCE
Hannah is a former journalist and filmmaker who currently works in media strategy at the House of Commons. She is an avid wild swimmer and former KLPA committee member. She has also done short and long distance walks all her life, including much of the Appalachian Trail and many remote trekking routes in the Western Himalaya.

PEPE PETOS
Pepe is a student and a filmmaker and is now travelling the world with his Froute project (www.froute.net) to raise money for UNICEF, UNESCO and the UNHCR.

MELANIE REED
Melanie is a product director, year-round pond swimmer and nature lover. Born and raised in South Africa, she spent a lot of her childhood in the bush and on the family's wildlife conservation farm. Hampstead Heath, the Kenwood Ladies' Pond and walks in nature provide her with a much-needed escape from the madness of the city.

SARAH SAUNDERS
Sarah is a photographer and winter swimmer who has been swimming in rivers and the sea since childhood. She runs a digital imaging and picture archiving consultancy, Electric Lane, and is grateful for the chance to leave her desk for the companionship, fun and sheer joy of running on the heath and swimming in the Ladies' Pond.

LYDIA SYSON
A former World Service radio producer, Lydia now writes historical, political novels for young adults (A World Between Us, That Burning Summer, Liberty's Fire), as well as other kinds of books. She and her large South London family love walking and wild camping. They hate chlorine.

ELIZABETH VALENTINE
Liz is an academic psychologist, author, editor and KLPA member. She has enjoyed regular country walks and swims in the Ladies' Pond for many decades but was only introduced to the delights of wild swimming while engaged on this project.

ARMORER WASON
Armorer works in international development, and has lived and worked in the vast open spaces of Mongolia, Siberia and Central Asia. Closer to home, walking and wild swimming help her connect with herself and feel part of the natural world.

OLGA WAY
Olga has enjoyed swimming since she was a girl and discovered the Ladies' Pond in 1983 when she came to live in London. Until then, she had swum in indoor pools and the sea, so the discovery of a freshwater pond was an unexpected find.

Copyright

Lead Editor:
Margaret Dickinson
Photo editors:
Sarah Saunders,
Graeme Cookson
Cover illustration:
James Lewis
Design and layout:
Sue Gent, Amy Bolt
Sub-editor:
Siobhan Kelly
Proofreading:
Michael Lee,
Liz Valentine, Anne Burley
Publisher:
Wild Things Publishing Ltd

wildthingspublishing.com

Acknowledgements:

This book owes its existence to the Kenwood Ladies' Pond Association (KLPA), to the members' enthusiasm and the committee's support. A small working group has played a key role. Mary Cane, Cath Cinnamon, Jo Goldsworthy, Sarah Saunders, Liz Valentine and, in the early stages, Melanie Reed and Olga Way, met regularly with me to plan, share out tasks and help take the many decisions involved in advancing from a concept to a book. Sarah Saunders has been a wonderful picture editor and a constant source of inspiration and encouragement. Liz Valentine used her keen critical skills to improve and correct much of the text. Jo Goldsworthy brought her experience of publishing to the project and was instrumental in finding our publisher.

I am extremely grateful to Anne Burley who went through the copy before submission and eliminated an embarrassing number of errors. Thanks also to Elizabeth Block who at an earlier stage helped with copy editing

The people who wrote up the walks, amended them and provided photographs are listed under Contributors and include a few who are evidently not KLPA members. It has been a great pleasure to see how their different interests and areas of knowledge inflect their walk descriptions. I am grateful to them for taking part and especially for appearing to enjoy themselves in the process.

Many more people – too many to name – helped indirectly by going on the walks, providing company, making suggestions and being photographed. I am not sure how many KLPA members went on a walk, but around 60 expressed interest. My own regular walking companions had little choice as I imposed 'book walks' on them, leant on them to take photographs or be photographed, and obliged non-swimmers to hang around while swimmers tested 'only one more quick swim'. I am thankful for their tolerance and their interest in pointing out that I had missed a good landmark, or just noted 'left' when in fact we had gone right.

I thank my husband, Jonathan Parry, for being a brilliant walking companion and for putting up with the working group periodically invading our kitchen. I owe much to my parents, HD and Sylvia Dickinson, who were keen walkers and swimmers and introduced my sister and me at a very early age to the joys of open countryside and cold water.

All of us involved in this project are indebted to campaigners past and present who have improved access for walking and swimming. The main campaigning organisations, the Ramblers, the River and Lake Swimming Association (RALSA), the Outdoor Swimming Society (OSS), have been important sources of information, as have the *Wild Swimming* books and website. We also referred to the Saturday Walkers' Club (SWC), a great organisation that I only discovered through one of our contributors. We are delighted to have worked with Daniel Start, from Wild Things Publishing, whose suggestions and comments have been extremely valuable. His involvement has been a big factor in the development of the book.

Photo credits:

All photos are copyrighted. p2 M Dickinson; p8 S Saunders; p10 top left & bottom left S Saunders, right M Dickinson; p11 S Saunders; p12 top left Liz Valentine, bottom left M Dickinson; p13 top right R Corney, bottom right Liz Valentine; p15 top right S Saunders, middle M Dickinson, bottom S Saunders; p17 left Liz Valentine, top right & bottom right S Saunders; p18 S Saunders; p19 left Lydia Syson, right Liz Valentine; p20 R Corney; p21 top, bottom R Corney; p22 R Corney; p23 left ,top right, bottom right S Saunders; p24&25 KLPA Archive; p2 R Corney; p28 R Corney; p30 S Saunders; p32 R Corney; p34 S Saunders; p37 top & bottom S Saunders; p3 S Saunders; p39 top & bottom S Saunders; p40 Cath Cinnamon; p42 all S Saunders; p44 top & bottom S Saunders; p46 M Dickinson; p48 all M Dickinson; p50 M Dickinson; p52 Natalie Start; p55 top Daniel Start, bottom M Dickinson; p56 M Dickinson; p57 M Dickinson; p58 S Saunders; p60 M Dickinson; p62 M Dickinso p65 top Maggie Jennings, bottom left & bottom right M Dickinson; p66 S Saunders; p68 top left Liz Valentine, top right S Saunders, bottom S Saunders; p72 S Saunders; p74 A Boulton; p76 top & bottom A Boulton; p77 A Boulton; p79 A Boulton; p80 A Boulton; p83 top A Boulton, bottom M Dickinson; p85 A Boulton; p86 S Saunders; p88 top & bottom S Saunders; p89 S Saunders; p91 left S Saunders, top right Liz Valentine, middle right A Bolton, bottom right S Saunders; p92 R Corney; p94 M Dickinson; p95 top R Corney, bottom M Dickinson; p97 M Dickinson; p98 Pepe Petos; p100 top left M Dickinson, top right & bottom Lydia Syson; p10 Liz Valentine; p106 top M Dickinson, bottom S Saunders; p112 S Saunders; p113 top & bottom S Saunders; p115 S Saunders; p116 S Saunders; p119 top & bottom S Saunders; p120 S Saunders; p122 Molly Fletcher; p124 Liz Valentine; p125 M Dickinson; p127 M Dickinson; p128 S Saunders; p130 all S Saunders; 130 top & bottom S Saunders; p131 S Saunders; p133 S Saunders; p134 Ros Bayley; p136 M Dickinson; p138 M Dickinson; p141 top & bottom M Dickinson; p143 M Dickinson; p144 M Dickinson; p146 M Dickinson; P147 top & bottom M Dickinson; p149 all M Dickinson; p150 S Saunders; p152 top & bottom S Saunders; P155 top & bottom S Saunders; p156 M Dickinson; p159 M Dickinson; p161 M Dickinson; p 162 M Dickinson; p165 top & bottom M Dickinson; 167 top & bottom M Dickinson; p168 M Dickinson; p171 top & bottom M Dickinson p174 M Dickinson; p177 top & bottom M Dickinson; p179 M Dickinson; p181 M Dickinson; p182 S Saunders p184 top & bottom S Saunders; p187 top & bottom S Saunders; p188 A Boulton; p190 top M Dickinson, bottom Kathrien Guenther; p193 top & bottom M Dickinson; p194 M Dickinson; p196 M Dickinson; p197 top & bottom M Dickinson; p198 M Dickinson; p200 M Dickinson; p202 top & bottom M Dickinson; p203 M Dickinson; p204 M Dickinson; p 206 Graeme Cookson; COVER FLAP front, top S Saunders, middle M Dickinson, bottom S Saunders; COVER FLAP back, top Maggie Jennings, middle M Dickinson, bottom R Corney. Many thanks to Graeme Cookson and to the women who took the pictures on page 110 and 113. A special thanks also to the two children on page 72 who were having their very first river swim.